OUTLINES OF SWISS HISTORY

« *What country can boast of having a purer and more heroic origin? What unrivalled images, what imperishable examples are not suggested by the simple, half-awed peasant opposed to the feudal horseman in his glittering panoply— the banished minority forgetting their wrongs in the hours of their country's peril—the peaceful magistrate devoting life and kindred to the safety of his fellow citizens —and the contempt of numbers when freedom was at stake?* »

STRATFORD CANNING.

SWITZERLAND, a small country of approximately four million inhabitants, covering an area of 15,950 sq. miles, is economically little favored by nature. One quarter of its soil is barren. It has no outlet to the sea and possesses practically no prime materials. The country is extremely mountainous and there are enormous differences of height ranging from 633 ft. above sea level on the shores of Lake Maggiore to 15,203 ft. in the Monte Rosa group. The

The lake-dwellers.

3

Vercingétorix.

Julius Caesar.

population is divided most un-
evenly betwen the twenty-two cantons. The canton of Berne, for
instance, has 729,000 inhabitants
while Appenzell Inner Rhodes has
only 13,000.

Switzerland is a country where
three cultures meet and where
four languages—German, French,
Italian and Romansch—are spoken
There are, however, only four Swiss
cities with a population of more
than a hundred thousand inhabitants : Zurich (336,000), Basel
(162,000), Berne (130,000), Geneva
(124,000). Yet despite its variety
and its limitations, Switzerland
has been able to derive strength
from weakness and spiritual enrich-
ment and harmony from diversity.

As far back as exact European
history can be traced—in the
case of Switzerland some two
hundred years B. C.——the country was inhabited by the Helvetians, a Celtic tribe who were
conquered by the Romans in
58 B. C. The Romans built military roads over various mountain
passes such as the St. Bernard,
Julier, Septimer and Splügen
passes. Their chief settlements
were at Aventicum (Avenches) in
the canton of Vaud, Vindonissa
near Brugg in the canton of Aargau, Augusta Rauracorum near

Basel, and Curia Rhaetorum (Chur) in the Grisons.

Later Huns, Burgundians, Alemanni and Ostrogoths swept through the peaceful Alpine valleys, settling in various parts of the country, so that the races became intermingled and in the Swiss of today there is a mixture of Celtic, Alemannic, Burgundian and Roman elements.

In the early Middle Ages, the country was christianized for the greater part by the Irish monks, Gallus and Fridolin, one of whom gave his name to the monastery and canton of St. Gall, the other of whom became the patron of the canton of Glarus.

In the course of time, the country became a part of the Holy Roman Empire and was ruled by bailiffs or nobles of the surrounding districts, such as the counts of Zähringen, Kyburg and Lenzburg as well as by the Dukes of Savoy. In the 12th century, the Habsburgs, who at that time had already become counts in Upper Alsace, inherited extensive properties in Aargau and in what was then known as the Zürichgau. Later Central Switzerland also fell under their sway, but, under Rudolph of Habsburg who ruled from 1273 to 1291, this district enjoyed a certain amount of

Foundation of the St. Gall Convent.

Charlemagne.

freedom. It was a different story, however, when his son, Albrecht, came to the throne. Consequently after the death of Rudolph, on the Ist of August 1291, representatives of Uri, Schwyz and Unterwalden met and formed a league for mutual safety and protection of their liberties against the new Austrian tyrant.

Infuriated by this act, Albrecht departed from the usual custom of naming a nobleman as protector or bailiff and instead sent to Switzerland men on whom he could rely to carry out his plans. Taxes were increased and the smallest offences were severely punished. The famous story of William Tell dates from this period. And Thomas Coryat, an Englishman, writing in 1611, describes this episode in language suitable to the spirit of the times : « When as the German emperors, being the lords of the principal cities of Helvetia, constituted foreign prefects and rulers, about three hundred years since as their deputies over three towns, it happened that the prefect of the town of Uri behaved himself very insolently, abusing his authority by immoderate tyrannizing over the people. For amongst other enormous outrages that he committed, he commanded one of his servants to compel all travellers that passed such a way to do reverence to his hat that was hung upon a staff

A Medieval Scene.

in the highway. The people, unwilling to offend the magistrate, did their obeisance. But one amongst the rest, even this foresaid William Tell, being a man of stout courage, refused to do as the rest. Whereupon he was brought before the magistrate who, being grievously incensed against him for his contu‑ macy, enjoined him this penance : that he should shoot an arrow out of a crossbow at an apple set upon his son's head. At first Tell refused, but at last, because he saw there was an inevitable necessity imposed upon him, he performed the matter greatly against his will, and that with most happy success. For God himself directing the arrow, he struck off the apple from the child's head without any hurt at all to the child. And whereas Tell had another arrow left besides that which he shot at his son, the prefect asked him what he meant to do with that arrow. Tell made him this bold and resolute answer : « If I had slain my child with the first, I would have shot thee through with the second. » The magistrate hearing that commanded him to be appre‑ hended and carried away in a bark. And when he was come betwixt the town of Urania and Brun, having by good fortune escaped out of the boat, he ran away with all possible expedition over the difficult places of the mountains, where there was no common way and so came to a place near to the one which he

William Tell.

knew the tyrant would pass, where he lay in ambush in a secret corner of the wood till he came that way, and then shot him through with his other arrow. »

In 1308 Emperor Albrecht was murdered by his own nephew and the Emperor, Henry VII, who was an opponent of the Habsburgs, allowed the Waldstatten, as they were then called, a certain independence. However, upon his death, persecutions by Austria again set in. On November 15, 1315, a force of 20,000 Austrians under Duke Leopold of Austria, a son of the murdered Albrecht, approached Morgarten in Schwyz. A small army of 1300 men from Uri, Schwyz and Unterwalden stationed themselves in the hills and, as the Austrians approached, started rolling rocks and boulders down on the invaders. In the general confusion which ensued, the Swiss attacked and in less than two hours 1500 Austrians were either killed or drowned while the remainder fled in terror. From this battle, Duke Leopold returned « pale, ashamed and in despair. »

During the next seventy years, five new cantons joined the Confederation : Lucerne (1332) Zurich (1351) Zug (1352) Glarus (1352) and Berne (1353).

The battle of Morgarten.

But the quarrels with Austria continued. Finally, in order « to finish once and for all with these rough peasants », Duke Leopold III, a nephew of the Leopold who had been defeated at Morgarten, assembled an army near Brugg. Certain German nobles swelled his forces and two hundred cavalry men were sent by the Duke of Milan. The first attack was planned against Lucerne and for that purpose the invaders marched via Zofingen to Sursee and then on July 9, 1386 to Sempach. Duke Leopold was so sure of victory that he himself rode out before the walls of Sempach to show the Austrians the rope with which he was going « to hang up the Swiss. » Shortly the approach of a Swiss army of about 1500 men drawn from Lucerne, Uri, Schwyz and Unterwalden was announced and the Austrian cavalry under the personal leadership of the Duke made ready for battle. While the Switzers, as they were then called, were praying to God and the Blessed Virgin that they might be delivered from their enemies, the Duke and his men formed a solid square and awaited the attack. With their long spears, they could prevent the Swiss, who were armed with, axes and halberds, from approaching

9

Arnold von Winkelried

closely. And it was at this point that Arnold von Winkelried of Unterwalden won undying fame for himself. Rushing against the Austrian lances, he clasped as many of them as he could in his arms and fell, pierced with many wounds. History has it that his words as he did this were : « Confederates, I will open you a path! Take care of my wife and children. » But the Swiss, ever mistrustful of theatrical gestures, have it that what he really cried as he fell was : « Who is the pig who pushed me ? »

The victory of Sempach greatly endangered Austrian prestige and two years later on April 9, 1388, a decisive battle was fought at Näfels in the canton of Glarus. Again the superior number of the enemy had forced the Swiss to retire to the mountains, but once again they were able to force the Austrians into a disastrous retreat.

In the battle of St. Jakob an der Birs (near Basel) in 1444, a Swiss advance-guard of 1500 soldiers fought against a French advance-guard of 20,000 Armagnacs under the Dauphin of France, killing more than half of the French while all the Swiss fell on the battlefield. The French prince was so impressed by the courage of the Swiss that he refused to advance any further into Switzerland. Instead he offered the Swiss a treaty of friendship which lasted down until the time of the French revolution.

Charles the Bold.

Between the years 1474 and 1478, the Swiss fought four battles against Charles the Bold, of Burgundy—at Héricourt (France) in 1474, at Grandson on the Lake of Neuchatel and at Morat in Fribourg in 1476 and again at Nancy (France) in 1477—thereby smashing the power of the Dukedom of Burgundy, the most dangerous enemy of Swiss independence at that time.

Throughout all these wars, the Swiss won a high reputation for military prowess, while their reputation for excellent markmanship has continued down to the present day. When Swiss military prowess was at its height, Switzerland was faced with deciding whether or not to become an imperialistic power. Her alliances, which were very much sought after, already linked her with princes and distant towns in the German empire, in Italy and in France. Such a policy, however, meant that the cantons would have to renounce much of their independence to a strong central government. And this they were not willing to do.

Profiting by this wise and historic decision on the part of the Swiss, the neighboring powers of France and Germany, as well as the Duke of Milan and others, enlisted more and more Swiss soldiers in their armies. This merce‹ nary service, although in many ways it brought great glory to the Swiss, eventually began to endanger the very existence of the Confederation. And

Nikolaus von der Flüe.

The battle of Marignano.

after the Italian mercenary wars of 1513-1515 in which, at the battles of Novara and Marignano, important forces composed of Swiss mercenaries faced each other, Switzerland decided to forbid her citizens from taking service as mercenaries and this prohibition remained in force nearly 200 years. Then in the 18th century several Swiss mercenary regiments under Swiss commanders served under the King of France. And it was members of a Swiss regiment who fell before the gates of the Tuileries in Paris in 1792 defending Louis XVI to the last. The only remnant of this mercenary service which still survives today—the only one allowed by federal law—is the Swiss guard at the Vatican consisting of some 200 men.

The period between the close of the Burgundian wars and the Reformation saw the appearance of two very different yet equally interesting figures on the Swiss scene—Nikolaus von der Flüe and Matthew Schinner.

Nikolaus was the son of a rich peasant family of Unterwalden who during his childhood performed his religious duties with an almost eccentric scrupulousness. He ate nothing on Fridays, and often fasted on other days. He seemed truly destined for holy orders. But instead he joined one of the armies fighting against Austria and eventually became a captain. However, suddenly at the age of fifty, he decided to renounce the world. Leaving his wife and ten children, he built a cell and a tiny chapel in the gorges of the Ranft, only about an hour from his home and retired to a life of solitude and prayer. Once a week he went to communion in a nearby village but that was all he ate. Neither the spies set about his cell by the authorities nor the emissaries of the Bishop ever caught him at fault. The legend of his piety grew. Pilgrims began coming to Ranft. His advice became all powerful and it was thanks to him that the Swiss, who were quarrelling over the spoils of the Burgundian wars, settled their disputes at the Diet of Stans in 1486.

Calvin.

Matthew Schinner was as worldly as Nikolaus von der Flüe was holy. A son of Valaisan peasants, he rose by sheer force of will and shrewdness to become a cardinal and statesman more powerful than the Pope and a great strategist in the bargain. His dream was a powerful state, centering in the regions around the Gotthard under the domination of the Swiss confederacy and comprising Lombardy,

Zwingli the Reformer.

13

Urs Graf, the painter.

Burgundy and Swabia. The military power of the Swiss at that time seemed to justify such a dream but had it succeeded it would have meant the end of the Confederation.

The years 1518-1536 brought the Reformation to Switzerland with Zwingli preaching in Zurich and Calvin in Geneva. But the central cantons which were predominantly rural, rejected this innovation and a period of religious quarrels and unrest set in. These religious quarrels were followed by clashes between the sovereign cantons and their bailiwicks, between city and rural populations, between the patrician classes and the people. It sometimes seemed as though the Confederation was on the verge of disruption. Yet it held together in spite of everything.

France of the Directory invaded and oppressed the country. Imperial France enslaved it and Switzerland had to wait until 1814 to regain her liberty. But at the Congress of Vienna, Swiss neutrality and independence were recognized by the European powers, all of whom realized it would be to their mutual interest to have a free and independent nation guarding the Alpine passes.

A new era of liberal thought and individualism now began. The 19th

Jürg Jenatsch

century was a wonderful period in Swiss history. The position of the State was consolidated and its economic structure developed. A final religious conflict broke out in 1847, strife with the Sonderbund, a secessionist move‑ ment of the Catholic cantons. But this civil war was quickly resolved by General Dufour and in the following year the constitution of 1848 firmly established the Confederation as it is today.

As for the Swiss people, John Ruskin, who knew Switzerland well, has probably given us the best description of their character.

« There has been much dispute respecting the character of the Swiss, aris‑ ing out of the difficulty which other nations had to understand their simpli‑ city. They were assumed to be either romantically virtuous or basely mer‑ cenary, when in fact they were neither heroic nor base, but were true‑hearted men, stubborn with more than any recorded stubbornness ; not much regar‑ ding their lives, yet not casting them causelessly away , forming no high idea of improvement, but never relaxing their grasp of a good they had once gained ; devoid of all romantic sentiment, yet loving with a practical and patient love that neither wearied nor forsook ; little given to enthusiasm in religion, but maintaining their faith in a purity which no worldliness deadened and

The end of the old Confederation.

Napoléon.

no hypocrisy soiled ; neither chivalrously generous nor pathetically humane, yet never pursuing their defeated enemies, nor suffering their poor to perish ; proud, yet not allowing their pride to prick them into unwary or unworthy quarrels ; avaricious yet contentedly rendering to their neighbor his due...

You will find among them no subtle wit nor high enthusiasm, only an undeceivable common sense, and an obstinate rectitude. They cannot be persuaded into their duties but they feel them ; they use no phrases of friendship but they do not fail you at your need. »

In Switzerland there are four so-called national languages, i.e., languages guaranteed by the Federal Constitution. Three of these languages are spoken in at least one whole canton. They are German, French, and Italian. Romansch, which was raised to the status of a national language in 1937, is widespread in the Grisons. German is spoken by nearly three million of Switzerland's four million inhabitants and is the language of the majority of the inhabitants of fourteen cantons. French is spoken by approximately eight hundred thousand people and is the official language of the three cantons Vaud, Neuchatel and Geneva. Italian is spoken by about two hundred and fifty thousand people and is the official language of the Tessin. Romansch is spoken by about fifty thousand people living in the Grisons, where it has an official character alongside German and Italian. In three cantons— Berne, Fribourg and Valais— where German and French are spoken by considerable parts of the population, both are the cantons' official languages.

French, German and Italian are the official languages of the Swiss Confederation. These three languages are equal and are spoken in the Swiss Parliament and in the Federal Tribunal. Every citizen and the authorities of each canton have the right to correspond in their own language with the Federal and cantonal authorities. Federal statutes and ordinances are published in French, in German and in Italian. All these texts are considered as originals and none may be regarded as being merely a translation of another.

Romansch is, with its two dialects —Surselva and Ladin, the latter spoken in the Engadine—a national, but not an official language. In this way the language of an important minority is guaranteed recognition without its use being compulsory in official business.

General Dufour.

Henri Dunant

This language is derived from Latin and has certain similarities with the Provencal spoken in the south of France. Through these various measures it has been possible to avoid language quarrels in Switzerland—quarrels which have so often disrupted other countries where several languages are used by the population.

From the religious standpoint, Switzerland presents the same lack of homo‑geneity. As far as religions are concerned, 57 % of the population is Protestant and 41 % is Catholic while the remaining 2 % is composed of various faiths. The Protestants are in a majority in twelve cantons, of which nine are German speaking and three French speaking. And the Catholics are in a majority in ten, of which seven are German speaking, three are partly French speaking and one is Italian speaking. Each of these creeds is equally protected in Switzerland. None is favored. None is forbidden.

DEMOCRACY
OF A
SMALL NATION

Bonfire celebrating national holiday.

« *Nature has made your State federal. To try to over‹
come her is not the part of wisdom.* »
(Napoléon in a speech to the Swiss Delegates in Paris
on December 12, 1802).

L ORD BRYCE, in his authoritative work « Modern Democracies », writes:
« The most interesting lesson Switzerland teaches is how tradition and
institutions, taken together, may develop in the average man, to an
extent never reached before, the qualities that make a good citizen —shrewd‹
ness, moderation, common sense and a sense of duty to the community. It
is because this has come to pass in Switzerland that democracy there is more
truly democratic than in any other country. »
It is difficult to gain an insight into the character and life of the Swiss people,

if one does not fully understand the importance attached to civic consciousness in this country.

Every citizen, even the most humble, is convinced that he has a personal responsibility towards the community which is,

Swiss elections.

in his eyes, the ultimate owner of his own spiritual and material heritage.

By definition and in fact, Switzerland is a federated state. Swiss political institutions rest on the fundamental principle of the sovereignty of the people. At every rung of the governmental administration there is not one man alone but a group of men.

The Federal Council, which constitutes the central executive power, is composed of seven members. They deal with all the business for the two houses of parliament, advise on legislation, prepare bills, etc. and carry out all administrative work. The individual members are elected at a joint meeting of the two houses, not by proportional representation. Each year one of them is chosen as President of the Confederation. But this is largely a nominal position. The President presides at meetings of the Federal Council, and must fulfil a few extra ceremonial duties. Actually, however, his influence is not different from that of any other

A Cantonal government.

Federal Councillor. Often even the politically minded Swiss do not know his name.

The state is governed by the Federal Assembly which consists of two separate and equal houses, the National Council, which has a number of members proportionate to the population—one deputy for every 22,000 electors —and the Council of States consisting of two members from each canton.

The Swiss have a deep loyalty to their cantons and nothing is as much resented as any attempt to increase the powers of the central government at Berne. There are twenty-two Swiss cantons : Zurich, Berne, Lucerne, Uri, Schwyz, Unterwalden, Glarus, Zug, Fribourg, Solothurn, Basel, Schaffhau-sen, Appenzell, St. Gall, Grisons, Aargau, Thurgau, Tessin, Vaud, Valais, Neuchâtel and Geneva. Three of these cantons are subdivided in sovereign half cantons : Unterwalden is divided into Obwalden and Nidwalden ; Appen-zell into Inner Rhodes and Outer Rhodes ; Basel into Basel Town and Basel Country.

Just as the canton is the basis of Swiss democracy, so is the self-governing commune, of which there are 3,107 in Switzerland, the basis of cantonal democracy. There is no tendency whatever to aggrandize the can-ton at the cost of the commune. The business of the canton is to control and co-ordinate the communes and to carry out such functions as they cannot deal with separately.

Swiss democracy has grown almost entirely from below, which perhaps explains why it is so healthy and well rooted. As Sir E. D. Simon points out : « The good fortune of the Swiss is that their history began among small groups of people living in secluded mountain valleys, who came together for

A musical Society.

common defence against foreign tyranny, and gradually built up the present communes and cantons and finally, based on these small and almost self-governing units, the national state. »

In the rural and more sparsely populated cantons of Unterwalden, Glarus and Appenzell, an ancient type of popular assembly, called the « Landsgemeinde » has still survived. In these cantons, the citizens as-

A rural communal council.

semble on the main square of the capital town to hear the reports submitted by their political representatives, to elect the latter and to vote new laws by a show of hands. This is pure, direct democracy as opposed to representative democracy in which people express their wishes through the intermediary of representatives or deputies entrusted with the conducting of public affairs. Throughout Switzerland, however, a mixed form of democracy, neither entirely pure nor entirely representative, is prevalent. Thanks to the initia-

Gymnasts coming back from a feast.

tive and referendum, the actual political rights of the Swiss people themselves are very extensive. There are two types of referendum—constitutional and legislative. The constitutional referendum is when the citizens have the final right to decide whether the constitution itself or amendments thereto shall be adopted or rejected. A legislative referendum is when this right is applied to laws. The constitutional referendum exists in all Swiss cantons and has also been adopted by the Confederation. It is always compulsory in both Federal and cantonal matters. The legislative referendum is provided by all the can, tons except those where the legislative power is exercised directly through the « Landsgemeinde ». It is sometimes compulsory, sometimes optional, or a combination of both as in the cantons of Geneva, Vaud, and Schwyz where it is compulsory for important financial laws, optional for other laws. The number of signatures necessary to provoke an optional referendum varies according to the canton. For instance, only 500 signatures are necessary in the small canton of Zug, whereas 6,000 signatures are required in the canton of Vaud. The legislative referendum is optional in all Federal matters and a request must bear the signatures of at least 30,000 citizens. Between 1848 and 1942, there were one hundred and thirty-six popular votes on Federal matters. Eighty-nine of them concerned constitutional amendments and in forty-six cases the amendment was passed while in forty-three it was rejected.

The Swiss people have showed a remarkable sanity of judgment in their use of the referendum and have applied it most opportunely to reject bills which were either too bureaucratic and infringed their liberties or were too onerous and exposed them to what might be termed financial adventures. The initiative, like the referendum, has both the constitutional and legislative form.

In contrast to the Confederation, the cantons have established a unicameral system which is sometimes known as the Cantonal Council but more often as the Great Council. The cantonal executive power is vested in a college of public officers known in French Switzerland as the « Conseil d'Etat » and in German Switzerland as the « Regierungsrat ».

But when we come to the communes we again find the government orga, nized more or less as a small scale state. The communes administer themselves, pass their own laws, elect their own council, levy their own taxes and choose their own executives. The communes in Switzerland are the real training school of democracy and the individual Swiss citizen, particularly in the smaller communes, manifest a tremendous interest in communal affairs.

THROUGH
TOWNS
and
CANTONS

BASEL

AND NORTHWEST SWITZERLAND

BASEL, situated near the German-French frontier, is known as "the gateway to Switzerland." Famed throughout the centuries for its philosophers, painters and mathematicians, it is at the same time a city with a rich commercial tradition. The people of Basel, although German speaking, possess a real touch of French esprit. This is clearly demonstrated in their yearly carnival, the most strikingly picturesque of all Swiss carnivals.

The Cathedral of Basel.

BASEL

*« The lower rank of citizens are in general so strongly
prejudiced in favour of their own country as to seem
convinced that true felicity is only to be found in Basel.»*
Rev. William Coxe.

BASEL (Bâle or Basle) is the capital of the half-
canton of Basel-Stadt, and is situated on the
Rhine near where three countries,—France,
Germany and Switzerland—meet. On one bank
lies Gross-Basel, with its Münster, Rathaus,
University, museums and private dwellings,
while on the other is Klein-Basel with its indus-
tries and the Badischer Bahnhof, used exclusively for traffic with Germany.

The people of Basel are very reserved and aloof. And it is said that for
the citizens of Basel, the best thing about Zurich is the afternoon train back
to Basel.

The Spalentor.

After gaining its independence in the early Middle Ages, the city acquired international fame after the Councils of Basel (1431-1448). It then became the residence of the most learned scholars and celebrated artists of the period. Art in Basel reached a high point in the 15th century in the work of such artists as Konrad Witz and Hans Holbein. And among the dominating personalities of this brilliant epoch were Erasmus of Rotterdam, the great humanist, who for many years lived and worked in the city. In 1501, in order to better protect herself against the covetous Austrian nobility, Basel joined the Swiss Confederation.

Aeneas Sylvius Piccolomini, who as Pope Pius II, founded the University of Basel has left us a description of the town in 1434 which conveys much of its real flavor. In a letter to a friend he writes of Basel as an enchanting place but regrets that the earthquake of 1335, which caused great conster-

The fair of Basel.

nation throughout the civilized world, destroyed much of the «old city.» He says the churches in Basel are built of red sandstone and that they contain small wooden cubicles, so that the ladies of the aristocracy may attend Mass unseen and undisturbed. Most of the churches and many of the private houses are roofed with tiles of colored glass which glitter in the sun. (This is still true of the Münster today.) Furthermore, most of the roofs are sloping and storks roost in the gables raising their young unmolested, due to a supersti-tion that it would bring bad luck to disturb them. The homes of the aristocracy are well built and luxurious with courtyards and foun-tains. They are warm and dry with windows of glass— a great rarity at that epoch. The streets are neither too wide nor too narrow and two carriages can pass abreast. The city's fountains are beautiful and picturesque but the fortifications hold out little hope of being able to withstand serious assault by a determined enemy. The strength of the town lies more in a moral quality and an inner harmony which would weld its citizens together in time of dan-ger. The population is well-behaved and de-pendable, preferring actually to be honest,

Basel, from the Rhine.

rather than just to seem so. They are decidedly not interested in foreigners and ask nothing more of life than their « freedom. »

The spirit of Basel is not very different today than it was five hundred years ago. But nobody can really understand the real nature of the Bâlois, or the true « esprit Bâlois, » who has not witnessed the city's yearly carnival with its metaphysical construction and its physical passion. At the time of the Grand Councils, the people celebrated carnival time largely by eating

In the zoological garden.

and drinking. But today the voice of the past is heard in a subtle combina‹ tion of wit, humor and sarcasm, expressed in pamphlets, processions, floats, masks and caricatures, dealing with every imaginable subject, political and otherwise, all to the accompaniment of an incessant beating of drums. In Basel, drumming has been raised to a fine art and entire concerts are given with nothing but drums.

M. D. Hottinger has described the Basel carnival thus :

« First Kleinbasel has her turn. One day in January, at eleven o'clock in the morning, there comes floating down the Rhine on a raft a strange figure, the Wilder Mann, the savage from the woods, crowned and girdled with fresh green and apples. Landing just by the Mittlere Brücke on the Klein‑basel side, he is welcomed by a lion and a griffin, the Lai and Vogel Gryff, and the three together perform a solemn dance in which gestures and steps are strictly prescribed. Then, accompa‑nied by the drums, they march to the exact middle of the bridge and perform their dance once more, then retire to pass the day junketing in Kleinbasel. »

« These strange figures are the insignia of the three guilds of Kleinbasel, which has always kept itself somewhat aloof from Grossbasel, and it must have been a charming sight when the great gate stood astride the bridge, to see the three dancing, their backs turned sedulously to the Lällenkönig, who stretched out his tongue at them. »

« The Carnival of Basel, however, is another matter. Groups are formed and costumes prepared in dead secret. These costumes are allusions to events and personalities of the day, and are by no means lenient in their satire. The leading personalities of Basel must, at carnival time, be armed with a good sense of humor, for they will not be spared. The year in which there is no fun poked at neighbor Zurich is specially noted in the annals of carnival. There is an intimate hostility between the two towns, very piquant to observe, which finds unres‑

The carnival of Basel.

tricted expression at carnival time. There are processions during the day, but it is at night that the fun reaches its height. In the small hours, the lights in the centre of the town are turned out. Then from the lanes which lead on to the market-place, group after group emerges to the sound of the drums and a mighty tattoo is beaten. Magnificent and huge painted lanterns are the only illumination, each group carrying its own, and the spectacle is really unique, for thus we can imagine a carnival in the long past times when the lanterns were not a sport, but a necessity. Then the crowd disperses to eat the succulent soup of roasted flour sacred to the morning of carnival. »

«That is not the end of carnival. There are more processions, balls, and gaieties of all kinds, and as long as it lasts, anybody may say anything to anybody else. The utmost freedom of speech prevails and woe to anybody who has offended his neighbor in the past year! Then, when it is all over, the costumes and the lanterns are put away and Basel relapses into her own peculiar tristesse.»

The Münster, an edifice of red sandstone, is situated on the highest point in town, with a splendid view out over the Rhine into Germany. It was seriously damaged by the earthquake in 1356, but was rebuilt and reconsecrated in 1365. Near the Münster lies the beautiful 15th century Residence of the Bishops, which is inwardly, as well as outwardly, a gem of gothic architecture and contains some very fine panelling. Also worthy of mention is the Barfüsser Kirche, erected in the 14th century and now containing the Historical Museum, with one of Switzerland's most important art collections, as well as furniture belonging to Erasmus of Rotterdam. One should not fail to visit St. Martinskirche, St. Albanskirche, St. Leonhardskirche and St. Peterskirche, with its lovely Louis XIV fountain, erected in 1779. Basel abounds in beautiful fountains, such as the Fischmarktbrunnen (1492), the Webernzunftbrunnen (1677), the lovely Barok-Brunnen in the Zerkindenhof and the Vier-Lindenbrunnen on the Steinentorstrasse (1758).

Figures of the carnival.

For those interested in architecture, Basel is a treasure house of gothic and 18th century art. The gothic period is represented by such houses as the Heusler'sches Haus (1539) St. Albanstrasse 34, the alte Hammerschmiede, St. Albantal 35, the Vorstadt Gesellschaftshaus, the Gasthaus zum goldenen Sternen, Aeschenvorstadt 44, the Hug-sche Haus, Klosterberg 21 as well as the houses Am Gemsberg and many others. In the Münsterplatz, which is one of the most beautiful squares in Switzerland, architecturally speaking, are to be found some especially fine examples of baroque architecture of the 18th century.

«Without hyperbole,» writes M. D. Hottinger «it may be said that the Münsterplatz in Basel is one of the loveliest squares in Europe. It must be approached from the south—either from the Rittergasse or the Münsterberg. Then with the great mass of the Münster immediately at hand, the flight of grave eighteenth century façades on the left, the chestnut trees shading Pisoni's fountain on the right and the perspective closed by the bold outline of the Schürhof and the Rollerhof, the Münsterplatz lies open in all its beauty. For centuries this has been a great open space—here the great tourneys took place in the Middle Ages; the Evil Carnival among them; here Pope Felix was crowned in the presence of the people; here Basel's history played itself out until it moved, not symbolically, but actually downhill to the Marktplatz. Here, until the Reformation, lived the canons of the Chapter; here was the humanist Thomas Platter's famous school, here, in the 18th century, the Basel merchants had their home, withdrawn from the turmoil of the market-place. »

« Much of the unique charm of this square is due to the absence of any apparatus of monumentality. No single mind planned it, it expresses the will of no ruler. When, in the eighteenth century the whole west side was rebuilt the architect gave to the three neighboring houses, the And-lauerhof, Gymnasium, and Mentelinhof, each its distinct character. No line is quite straight here, no angle a right angle, not one roof line follows the rest, yet there is no impression of restlessness. No striking outward decor-ation distracts the eye from the fine sense of space. The touch of personality, of apparent hazard in the arrangement, which yet contributes to a general impression of harmony, is the natural expression of an individualistic people. »

« The same might be said of the corresponding district on the other side of the town, of such streets as the Nadelberg or the Obere Heuberg. The houses of the Nadelberg are withdrawn behind high walls. Here it is possible to see that Basel has always been somehow on the defensive. The streets of these quarters are tranquil even now : yet, with their quiet beauty, the sense of centuries of elegant living incorporated in them, they give an impres-sion of rare distinction. There is many a lovely courtyard with a fountain to be glimpsed through open doors, and where the house is in the hands of a public body, the owners are generally courteous enough to let the inquiring stranger in ».

Basel has also some very fine modern buildings, such as the new Bürgerspital, the largest hospital in Switzerland. Basel is also a medical centre and the seat of the Swiss Academy of Medecine. Furthermore there is a Tropical Institute

Niklaus Manuel Deutsch. The judgment of Paris.
(Museum of Basel.)

Olden houses near the Cathedral.

here which makes a point of studying tropical diseases as well as general conditions in tropical countries.

The Kunstmuseum, built especially to house Basel's fine collection of paintings, contains works of such masters as Holbein, Konrad Witz and Urs Graf as well as a whole floor dedicated to the works of Arnold Böcklin and other 19th century artists.

There is also in Basel, which is the centre of the Swiss chemical industry, a little known, but very interesting Pharmaceutical museum which the traveller should not fail to visit. It is installed in a gothic house, which forms part of a modern chemical laboratory and contains rooms of pharmaceutical products of every century, beginning with the laboratories of the alchemists.

The University of Basel is the oldest in Switzerland. It was founded by Pope Pius II shortly after the great Church Councils of Basel and opened its doors on April 4, 1460 in a humble building on the left bank of the Rhine which served as its headquarters until 1939. Today the new and handsomely equipped university buildings stand on the Petersplatz. The history of the university has been stormy and eventful. World famous scholars have taught here, including Oekolampadius, Paracelsus, Nietzsche and Jakob Burckhardt. At times the very existence of the university was threatened by religious conflicts such as the Reformation, political troubles, such as the Burgundian Wars or the French revolution and quite especially by the separation of the city of Basel from its rural districts in 1833. Yet the citizens of Basel have always felt deeply attached to their university and all difficulties have

always been overcome by the generosity and self-sacrifice of the people.

Plutocracy and learning have never been really separated in Basel as they were in Zurich, and among the names of Basel's patrician or industrial and merchant families have been some of her greatest savants. The name for learning which Erasmus helped to win for Basel was carried into the 19th century by two names of European distinction. The first is that of J. J. Bachofen. Long before the psycho-analytical schools of thought, he had realized the vigor of the irrational elements in the human psyche. Contemporary with him was Jakob Burckhardt, a historical philosopher of

the first order, gifted for the historical past with the same penetrating insight as Bachofen had for the past which has left no written history. While these men were working in Basel, there came to the staff of the university a young man, thirty years their junior, who for a time had the privilege of their friendship— Friedrich Nietzsche. For ten years he worked in Basel, and these years can be counted as not the least glorious moment of Basel's spiritual history. It was clear that the destroyer of all tradition must come into

In the Arlesheim grottoes.

violent conflict sooner or later with the profound conservatism of such men as Bachofen and Burckhardt and the Basel spirit in general, but as a his‹ torical fact, the presence in the one small town—Basel's population then was well under a hundred thousand— of three spirits of such dimensions is proof of that high care for spiritual things which is her abiding sign in history.

Even today the inhabitants of the half‹canton, Basel‹Stadt, are annoyed that in the year 1833 another half‹canton, Basel‹Land, was formed, for thereby they lost not only economic returns form agriculture but large forests as well. A third of the canton of Basel‹Land is forest.

An interesting excursion is to Arlesheim with its quaint baroque church, one of the most interesting churches of its kind in Switzerland. Not far from here is Dornach with its ultra modern academy of Anthroposophy. Also there are pleasant excursions into the Birsig valley, with the picturesque village of Binningen and its old church, St. Margaret, from where there are some splendid views. And not far from here is Flüh, a small village with mineral springs and a steep crag on which stands the Benedictine Abbey of

Mariastein, founded in 1645, a famous pilgrimage centre with its rock cavern of Maria-am-Stein.

Aarau, the capital of the canton of Aargau, lies on the right bank of the Aare river at the foot of the Jura. The Bally shoe factory, with its unique shoe museum, has made the name of Schonenwerd famous in the manufacturing world. And in the cantonal library there is Zwingli's Bible with marginal notes in the great reformer's own handwriting. This city has always produced the highest quality mathematical instruments and the finest bells.

A tour through this city which has a very marked character of its own, is best concluded by a visit to the Trade Museum, containing the stained-glass windows from the colonnade of Muri Convent, and a very interesting collection of paintings.

In the lower Aare valley a trip to the ancestral castle of the Habsburgs is a favorite excursion from Brugg, and the stately castle of Wildegg, not far distant from here, affords a splendid view. Among the numerous other castles in the canton of Aargau, mention must be made above all of Lenzburg,

The Castle of the Habsburg

Aarburg and Hallwil Castles. It is in the picturesque little town of Lenzburg that the famous Lenzburg jams and preserves are made.

A motor trip should be made through the charming little towns of Rhein/felden, Laufenburg, Kaiserstuhl, Zurzach, Zofingen Mellingen and Brem/garten, the latter of which with its old walls and its river is one of the most picturesque towns in Switzerland. Baden, which is an all year round spa, as well as a flourishing modern town where the Brown Boveri works are located, should be visited together with its lofty tower and its historical Assembly Room in the Council Hall.

Klingnau on the Rhine.

The traveller interested in art and history should also visit the once powerful monasteries of Königsfelden, Muri and Wettingen, for they are of great artistic and historical importance. Königsfelden is renowned throughout Europe. It was erected on the spot where the ruins of Roman Vindonissa were found and where King Albrecht I was murdered in 1308. The well preserved Gothic Monastery Church contains a set of impressive stained/glass windows in the choir which are considered among the best achievements of the 14th cen/tury. The nucleus of the Monastery Church at Muri is an Early Roman building whose nave was altered into a solemn central hall in 1700, and further adorned in 1750. At Wettingen, near Baden, the Early Gothic Monastery

Church was furnished with its famous choir pews and stucco-reliefs about 1600, and in 1760 its rich baroque adornment was added. The colonnade at Wettingen, with its mingled Gothic and rounded arches, is the only one in Switzerland that has preserved its rich treasure of 182 stained-glass windows from the 16th and 17th centuries.

Olten, one of the busiest railway centers in Switzerland and Solothurn, the capital of the canton are the two cities in the canton of Solothurn.

In the year 272 A. D. when the Alemanni threatened the Romans, a fortification was erected on the river Aare where the city of Solothurn now stands. A legend relates that two of the early Christians, Orsus and Victor, who had fled to Solothurn, were tortured and put to death because of their faith. The Cathedral of St. Ursus at Solothurn, built by Pisoni in 1762-73 is dedicated to their memory. This cathedral is one of the finest specimens of late Italian Renaissance in Switzerland.

Solothurn was once the residence of the French Ambassadors to the ancient Swiss Confederation and during this period the city was a center of diplomatic and cultural life. The main street runs from east to west towards the cathedral. Not far from here is the Jesuit Church, originating from early baroque times and perhaps even more interesting than the cathedral architecturally. The Council Hall contains a stairway where formerly the official receptions of the Ambassadors were held. On both sides there are fine architectural features in Renaissance style and in addition, a highly artistic spiral stair in a special turret staircase. Other striking buildings are the imposing arsenal with its fine collection of weapons and numerous patrician houses in the town and its immediate surroundings. Among these in the direction of Olten we find Schonenwerd Abbey, Bechburg Castle near Oensingen and the romantic ruins at Alt, and Neu-Falkenstein.

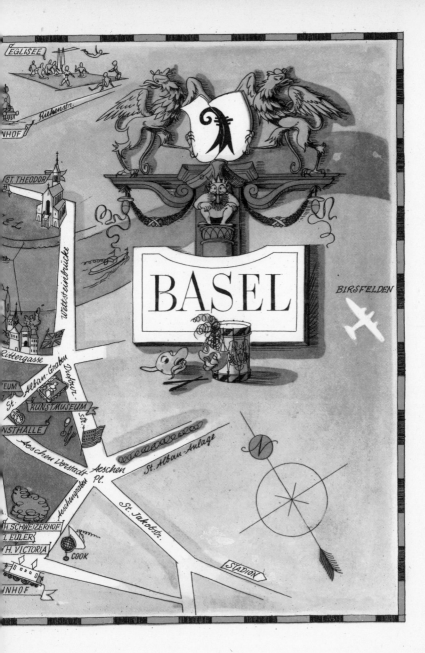

GASTRONOMY

E VER since the Middle Ages, Basel has been famous for its excellent food. Old-fashioned Basel cooking was, like German cooking, heavy and rich in fats. This made it particularly well-suited to the climate, which is inclined to be cloudy and gray.

Soups are a Basel specialty. Among the best known of these are « Durch-getriebene Hirnsuppe, » which con-sists mainly of brains passed through a sieve, to which have been added butter, flour, yolks of eggs and broth. This soup is served with «croutons» and can be made with hare and game of all kinds. « Klöschensuppe » is also a favorite and the « Klöss »—dumpling or meat ball—can be made out of meat, chicken, fish, or crab. Sweet soups are typical of the region and are prepared with wine, beer, grape juice, cherries and even chocolate!

Fish is well liked in Basel, especially the fine Rhine salmon, which is excellent smoked. The favorite way of cooking this salmon is to cut it in finger sized pieces after it has been scraped and cleaned. The slices should then be dried with a clean cloth, rubbed with salt and pepper, sprinkled lightly with flour, placed in a frying pan and browned in butter. When the meat of the fish begins to pull away from the bones, the slices should be carefully removed to a warm platter. More butter should be added to the butter in which the fish was fried, and one or two not too finely cut-up onions should then be browned in it. This butter should then be poured over the fish; followed by some broth which has been heated in the same pan in which the fish has been cooked.

Carp and small river crabs are also considered a great delicacy.

Basel produces fine hams and the « Klöpfer » sausage, a brand of « cervelas » sausages, are delicious. Wild boar is considered the greatest delicacy and is often available, due to the many forests around Basel. The meat of the wild boar is black and the animal should not be eaten after it is a year old. Wild pig is usually prepared as a « civet »—like jugged hare—or served stuffed.   Venison is also very popular here, just as it is in all parts of Switzerland during the hunting season.

During the « Fastnacht » carnival the whole population eats « Gebrannte Mehlsuppe, » made with burnt flour, and a pie called « Zwiebelwähe, » as well as small cheese cakes.

« Basler Leckerli, » a leathery kind of ginger cookie, and « Basel Pfannku⁄chen, » are the well known pastries.   Basel is also famous for its cherries, from which Basel Kirsch is made.

A hundred years ago the vineyards of the canton of Basel were nine times their present size.   The wine districts are divided into two parts : the « obere Baselbiet » producing the well⁄known blue burgundy, as well as the Buuser, Wintersinger and Maispracher wine, equal to the best red wines of the Zürich and Schaffhausen districts, and the « untere Baselbiet » in which are the two wine growing centres of Muttenz and Pratteln, overlooking the Rhine.   The Birstal produces the Münchensteiner, Arlesheimer, Reinacher, Kluser, and Pfeffinger wines, which are more like Alsatian wines.   In the Birsigtal are to be found the excellent wines of Therwil, Biel, Benken.

NEUCHATEL AND THE JURA

THE Jura Mountains, although less impressive than the Alps, have a melancholy beauty all their own with their stately pine woods and their wind-swept summits where cattle graze during the summer months. Neuchatel, with its exclusive old families, is the capital of the canton. Its cultural and aristocratic tradition is in sharp contrast to both the socialistic atmosphere of La Chaux-de-Fonds and the modern commercialism of Bienne. In this countryside lies the centre of the Swiss watch-making industry. Here also there is wine growing, horse-breeding and agriculture.

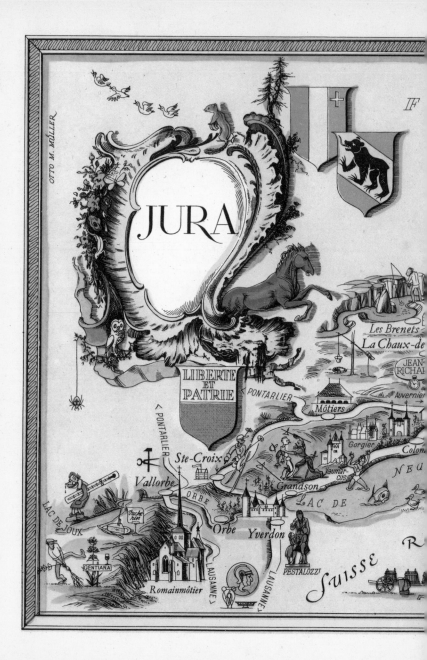

The « *Pierre Pertuis* ».

« *We saw the mighty Jura opposing its dark side to the ambition that would quit its native country, and an almost insurmountable barrier to the invader who should wish to enslave it.* »
MARY GODWIN SHELLEY.

THE canton of Neuchatel and the Jura mountains, although displaying great charm and diversity, are among the less known parts of Switzerland. The countryside comprises three different, yet well-defined types of landscape, each with its special charm, local interests, economy, aspirations and problems.

French is the common language, except for small German speaking settlements in the northern part of the canton. The French spoken in Neuchatel is

55

the purest spoken in Switzerland and is even admired by the French themselves.

There is the so-called low country, a long narrow strip of land between the lake of Neuchatel and the first hills. Then come the valleys, cut deep into the mountains, like the Val-de-Travers, through which the defeated Bourbaki army retreated from France in 1871 to seek refuge in Switzerland, or open plateaus like the Val-de-Ruz which again received regiments of a defeated French army in 1940.

The Jura mountains reach an altitude of between 4200-4800 feet. Their slopes are covered with dark pine forests, but their peaks are bare and wind swept. The majestic regularity of these mountains changes slightly in the north but without detriment to the picturesque severity and impressive, seductive melancholy of the countryside. The valleys and highlands are wild and often deserted except for the echo of cowbells. The towns and villages are small but there are plenty of inns and hotels to give a hearty welcome to the tourist. Life is hard in the Jura. The summers are short, the winters long and the cold, clear north wind—« la bise »— blows a great deal of the time. There is also a local wind known as the Joran which sweeps down from

Blauenstein.

the Jura, causing sudden squalls on the lake of Neuchatel and making it very treacherous for sailing. However, despite the fact that life is hard in the Jura, the Neuchatelois know how to enjoy themselves when the day's work is done.

It was in the Jura mountains that Hans Andersen wrote some of his loveliest fairy tales and it was here that the First International was started. In a little village at the foot of the Jura, there is a mill called the « Middle of the World », because from its mill pond flow two streams, one into the Aare and the Rhine, the other into the lake of Geneva and the Rhone. When Germany declared war in 1914, the miller closed the sluice gate which

56

A landscape in the Jura.

led to the Rhine, announcing quite simply : « They shan't have any water in Germany! »

Neuchatel, the capital of the canton, is a small, picturesque city with its yellow sandstone buildings making it seem, as Alexander Dumas said, « as if it were carved out of butter. » Neuchatel was among the last cantons to join the Swiss Confederation, but in 1848 it finally overthrew its last sovereign who, curiously enough, happened to be a Hohenzollern, although the canton is so definitely French in feeling.

Neuchatel still offers the visitor many vestiges of its eventful past when first it belonged to the ducal house of Orleans-Longueville, then to the Kings of Prussia and lastly gained its political independence. Following the Swiss tradition of mercenary service, many Neuchatel aristocrats served under the King of Prussia. And a regiment from Neuchatel took the city of Seringapa-tam for the British East India Company. There has always been a definite international tradition among the old families of Neuchatel. A member of the Pourtales family helped found Colorado Springs over a century ago, another was German ambassador to Petrograd and many members of the

family served in the French army. In the Second World War, several sons of old Neu-chatel families were killed fighting as volun-teers in the Royal Air Force.

The Neuchatelois have a special way of thinking and of speaking. They are alert diplomats and extremely conscious of their culture. But they have a definite feeling of superiority and are convinced that, as far as the important things in life are concerned, the world begins and ends within the con-fines of their canton. Yet although they are even more famous for their grumbling than other Swiss, they know how to extricate themselves from any kind of trouble.

Neuchatel, this lovely town where the charms of the lake, the gardens, and the old houses are enchantingly combined, is essentially a town of study. It has a university, several high schools and many boarding schools. From the shady quayside on sunny, clear days there is a magnificent panorama of the Alps, beginning with the Bernese chain and ending with Mt. Blanc in the far distance.

The University of Neuchatel comprises four faculties : theology, juris-prudence, philosophy and science. Although the means at the dis-

posal of the canton are not suffi-cient to maintain a medical facul-ty, the faculty of science prepares students for the preliminary di-ploma in medicine, pharmacology and dentistry. There is also a University School for teachers of French, a Department of Econo-mics and Commercial Science, and Chemical, Physical and Zoolo-gical Institutes.

A fruitful collaboration also arises from the close connection maintained with the Cantonal Observatory and the Swiss Labo-

St. Ursanne in the Bernese Jura.

ratory of Research in Watch Making. Despite its size, Neuchatel is remarkable for its intellectual life and for that reason it is often visited by leading theatrical companies and famous musicians.

Neuchatel also has its beach, its golf course, its tennis courts and ski and bob runs at Chaumont. In pleasant contrast to the more modern sections of the city is the delicate elegance of the Faubourg de l'Hôpital with its 18th century houses. The Hôtel du Peyrou in particular is an architectural jewel. There is also the graceful Maison des Halles and the Chateau, today the seat of the government, which together with the Collegiale—half Romanesque, half Gothic—crowns the small hill in the heart of the city.

Along the lake in the direction of Geneva are ancient towns, most of them with their own castle, surrounded by vineyards : Auvernier, Colombier, Boudry, Gorgier, Vaumarcus.

Entering the Val⁄de⁄Travers by way of the impressive Areuse gorges, there are larger villages : Travers, Couvet, Môtiers, Fleurier, St. Sulpice, Les Ver⁄ rières. Industry dominates the economy of this region(watches, machines, sewing machines, asphalt mines, etc.)

To the southwest, in the Jura Vaudois, lies the town of Ste. Croix, a summer resort and winter sport place with a beautiful view of the Alps. In this neighborhood, peat is cut where the soil is too poor to cultivate. But the main source of income for the comparatively small population is the raising of cattle and the production of cheese. In addition, the village folk do a little watch making, as well as manufacture music boxes, typewriters and small tools. There is also a certain amount of timber trade, fishing and breaking of ice in the small lakes of Joux and Brenet. The green surfaces of these two lakes, in the midst of a darkly beautiful countryside, produce an atmosphere of subtle melancholy reminiscent of Scandinavia. This countryside, far from the great cities, amidst an unfriendly nature, has an ancient civilization all its own. It dates back to the time when monks settled here towards the beginning of the 16th century, if not earlier. The monasteries have now disappeared. But at Romainmôtier, a fascinating, ancient town, there is one of the finest Romanesque churches in Switzer⁄ land.

In the Val⁄de⁄Ruz, on the route from Neuchatel to La Chaux⁄ de⁄Fonds, agriculture is of greater importan⁄ ce than industry. But watch making flourishes in the villages along the

railway line : Cernier, Fontaine,
melon, Les Hauts,Geneveys and
Les ˙Geneveys,sur,Coffrane.

La Chaux,de,Fonds is the world
centre of watch,making.   In the
Jura, the watch,making industry
developed extremely rapidly from
small beginnings. In 1679, at la
Sagne, an English watch in need of
repair fell into the hands of a lock,
smith's apprentice named Daniel
Jean Richard, who had a gift for
mechanics. Not only did Richard
understand how to repair the ins,
trument, but with tools which he
had made himself, he was able to
produce a watch of his own in a year
and a half. In 1705 he moved to
Le Locle where he taught his art to
his brothers and sons. All of a
sudden a dormant talent for inven,
tion sprang to life among the popu,
lation and everyone began making
watches. Some people claim it was
because the watch with its outer
precision and inner restlessness is so
peculiarly suited to the tempera,
ment of the people of this region.

La,Chaux,de,Fonds is the largest
town in the Swiss Jura. It is very
modern and has often been compa,
red with American cities of similar
size. In contrast to Neuchatel, the
tradition of La Chaux,de,Fonds has
always been socialistic. It was here
that Lenin lived during part of his
exile.   The climate is very dry and

Daniel Jean Richard

FONDATEUR DE L'HORLOGERIE DU JURA

Romainmôtier.

healthy, but severe. And the population, known for their jovial spirit, claim that they have «six months winter and six months taxes. » La/Chaux/de/Fonds was the home of Numa Droz who became Federal Councillor at the age of thirty/two and was Foreign Minister at the time of Bismarck. And it was in La/Chaux/de/Fonds that the movement for Neuchatel to throw off the yoke of Prussia and to join the Swiss Confederation started. The arts, especially painting and music, have always flourished here. The independent, if not revolutionary, spirit of the Jurassien has also made itself felt in painting in the work of Leopold Robert, in music through the work of Jacques Dal/croze and in architecture through the work of Le Corbusier.

In the lower part of the same valley as La/Chaux/de/Fonds lies Le Locle. The town clusters around an old church and watches and chocolate are made here. The population of Le Locle is supposed to be very temperamental. And the story goes that a woman of Le Locle, known as Marianne du Cre/

Vaillant, put a whole party of Burgundians to flight in the 15th century by letting the village bull loose.

On the Doubs river which forms the frontier between France and Switzerland, lies the charming village of Les Brenets. On one side is a lovely sort of fjord and on the other is the waterfall, Saut-du-Doubs, from where the Doubs continues its course through a number of wild gorges.

Going northwest from Neuchatel, the Bernese Jura opens out into endless valleys and forests. This is a splendid countryside for hiking and the lake of Bienne offers endless opportunities for sailing, swimming and fishing. Along the lake of Bienne, there is one village after another hidden among vineyards. Neuveville, a picturesque little town with its old towers and famous schools, is situated at the foot of the Chasseral, facing the idyllic island of St. Pierre where Jean Jacques Rousseau wrote his « Contrat Social » which served as an ideological basis for the French revolution.

Bienne, a very modern city of about forty thousand inhabitants, is a centre of industry. (watches, machines, motorcycles, automobiles, pianos, soap, etc.). Its inhabitants like to call it « the town of the future », but there are many quaint remnants of the past as for instance the houses on the Place du

Neuchâtel.

Soleure.

Marché. Bienne lying on the language frontier of French and German/speaking Switzerland, is a bi/lingual city. And it is very amusing to hear even the children mixing their languages.

Leaving Bienne by way of the Suze gorges past the Taubenloch waterfall, one enters the real Jura at St. Imier, the largest town in the valley. St. Imier is a watch making centre, guarded on one side by the Chasseral and by Mont Soleil on the other. From both of these mountains there are splendid views of the Alps and on both of them there is skiing in winter.

Delémont is the administrative, judicial and economic center of the Bernese Jura.

Here agriculture and industry are harmoniously combined without changing the ancient character of the town, with its castle, its 18th century Town Hall and its medieval doorways and fountains.

To the west lies the Clos/du/Doubs, where this slow flowing stream widens into a basin bordered by forests and rocky cliffs. Here lies the town of Ste.

Ursanne with its houses forming a rampart behind which stands its beautiful Romanesque church.

From now on the mountains decline rapidly into the hilly, fertile country of the Ajoie. Porrentruy, formerly residence of the Bishops, masters of the entire Bernese Jura, is the centre of this countryside. The French revolution brought the end of this regime and Porrentruy itself became the capital of the ephemeral «Departement du Mont Terrible» until this part of the Jura was incorporated into the canton of Berne.

Returning by the route of the « Corniche du Jura », where at Les Rangiers, facing the French frontier, stands a gigantic statue of a Swiss soldier, which commemorates the guarding of the frontier by the Swiss Army in 1914-1918, one reaches the Franches Montagnes with their high pine trees and their wide pastures. The Franches Montagnes are a famous horse breeding district, quite unlike any other part of Switzerland. Saignelégier is the main town of this district where the Doubs river flows through winding gorges. Here each year horse races and an important horse market are held which are visited by horse lovers from all over Switzerland and even from far beyond the Swiss frontiers.

GASTRONOMY

THE whole Jura countryside from Geneva to the tip of the Bernese Jura has a tradition of excellent cooking, naturally largely influenced by the cooking in the neighboring French countryside.

The lake of Neuchatel is famous for its fish—particularly the bondelle which is to be found in this lake alone and which is served deliciously in the inns at Auvernier with a sauce remoulade. Here, in these inns, with their flower-decked terraces, one also finds the brochet and the palée as well as the trout, usually served « au bleu, » which are so abundant in the mountain streams.

A Neuchatel specialty is « tripes à la Neuchateloise, » which means that the tripes are cooked for eight to ten hours in water to which has been added a few tomatoes, some onions, leeks, a few cloves, and a dash of lemon. The tripes are then removed from the water and served with a strong sauce vinaigrette, an ordinary French dressing to which chopped chives, onions, parsley, and chopped hard-boiled eggs have been added, and plain boiled potatoes.

Two kinds of sausages, the « saucisson » and the «saucisse au foie»—a kind of mild liver sausage—are also specialties of this countryside and are particularly good when cooked in the same kettle with finely cut-up leeks and potatoes. These sausages are also good when cooked with cabbage or with string beans and a favorite meal is to serve these sausages cooked with any of these particular vegetables and potatoes, the whole prepared in the same casserole.

The fondue is very popular in Neuchatel and is made with the wine of the countryside and a dash of native kirsch—that of Bèroche or of Ajoie. The usual recipe for fondue is as follows : An earthenware casserole is rubbed with garlic; then a deciliter of white Neuchatel wine is heated in the casserole; to this is added 125 grams of finely cut cheese—Emmentaler or Gruyère or a mixture of both—and the whole is stirred until the cheese is melted. The casserole is then removed from the fire, placed on the table over a spirit lamp, and each guest is served a portion of bread cut into small cubes which he or she dips into the fondue on the end of a fork. This process continues until the whole fondue is eaten.

In the canton of Neuchatel it is customary for the various bakeries to prepare a delicious type of small cheese tart each Monday. And in all the villages of the Jura, the housewives take their large tarts of rhubarb, plums or apricots, according to the season, which they have prepared at home, to the village bakeshop to be baked. Often the people of this countryside make their evening meal entirely from a cup of coffee and a large piece of one of these delicious and nourishing tarts.

The « vacherin du Jura, » a white creamy, soft cheese, somewhat suggestive of a mild camembert, is popular not only in this countryside but throughout Switzerland. The Bernese Jura also produces a tasty round cheese called the « tête de moine » (monk's head) cheese, and originally fabricated by the monks of Bellelay.

Neuchatel wines are apparently mild, but their mildness is as treacherous as the winds of the lake. Most Neuchatel wines are white, slightly sour and form a star when poured correctly. A very good red wine, however, is produced at Cortaillod. Two good brands of Neuchatel white wine are « Château d'Auvernier » and « Domaine de Champreveyres. » And a very good champagne—«Mauler »—is grown in this canton.

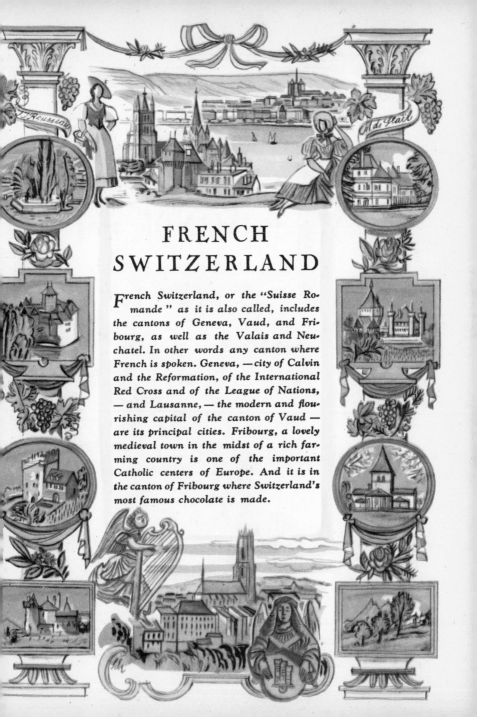

FRENCH SWITZERLAND

French Switzerland, or the "Suisse Romande" as it is also called, includes the cantons of Geneva, Vaud, and Fribourg, as well as the Valais and Neuchatel. In other words any canton where French is spoken. Geneva, — city of Calvin and the Reformation, of the International Red Cross and of the League of Nations, — and Lausanne, — the modern and flourishing capital of the canton of Vaud — are its principal cities. Fribourg, a lovely medieval town in the midst of a rich farming country is one of the important Catholic centers of Europe. And it is in the canton of Fribourg where Switzerland's most famous chocolate is made.

SUISSE
ROMANDE

LIBERTÉ
ET
PATRIE

FRAN

< PONTARLIER

Vufflens

Morges

Rolle

Nyon

< DIJON

LÉMAN

LAC

THONON >

Coppet

DUNANT

CHAMONIX >

RHONE

GENÈVE

< LYON

CALVIN

Dufour

J.Rousseau

F

R

A

Geneva.

LAKE LEMAN

« *Clear, placid Leman! Thy contrasted lake,*
With the wild world I dwelt in, is a thing
Which warns me, with its stillness, to forsake
Earth's troubled waters for a purer spring. »
Lord Byron *in* « *Childe Harold's Pilgrimage.* »

L AKE LEMAN, sometimes called the Lake of Geneva, has always had a tremendous attract‚ ion for poets and writers of all nationalities. It was on its shores, by Montreux, that J.J. Rousseau placed the unhappy love story of « La nouvelle Héloïse ». And Lord Byron always found solace for his distracted nerves in the silence of « clear, placid Leman. »

The surface of Lake Leman, reflecting on the north the sloping vineyards

The J. J. Rousseau monument in Geneva.

of the canton of Vaud, and on the south the chestnut groves and pastures of Savoy, is 1220 ft above the level of the sea. Its area of 224 sq. miles makes it the largest lake in Switzerland, while the Rhone, descending from the Valais, furnishes it with 70 % of its water, drawn from a surface of many hundreds of square miles of glaciers and snow. Yet Lake Leman itself never freezes except in certain small, very restricted areas.

Consequently there is a fairly southern type of climate on its shores, and the powerful radiations from its surface in autumn help ripen the grapes in the vineyards. This is one important reason why in this countryside all other crops have been sacrificed to the vine.

Along the lakeside between Geneva and Lausanne lie charming villages and lovely country estates. Several of the villages, such as Nyon, Rolle and Morges, have their own castles and any one of them provides an ideal setting for a quiet and restful vacation.

GENEVA

« *Geneva is too well known to be much insisted upon.* »
Bishop Gilbert Burnet writing in 1685.

The name of Geneva appears for the first time in Julius Caesar's « De Bello Gallico » : « Extremum oppidum Allobrogum est proximumque Helvetiorum finibus, Genava, » thus proving that the city is well over two thousand years old.

In 888 the second Burgundian kingdom, east of the Jura, was founded on the ruins of the Carlovingian Empire and Geneva became one of its chief towns. However, the Dukes of Savoy were interested in gaining power over Geneva.

And for centuries the struggle continued. Today on December 11th, the Genevese still celebrate, with festivities and processions, the anniversary of the Escalade, the day on which they repelled the last attempt by the Dukes of Savoy to conquer the town. Little pots made of nougat candy are eaten in memory of Mère Royaume who made the first enemy warrior fall back off the town wall by flinging a pot of rice soup at his head.

During the 18th century, Geneva basked in the glow emanating from the reputation of Voltaire who lived in a country house near Ferney and quarrelled with the leading figures of the period from there. Another man who lent prestige to Geneva at this epoch was Jean Jacques Rousseau, « citizen of Geneva », the brilliant son of a St. Gervais watchmaker. There were also many distinguished Frenchmen and Englishmen living in Geneva in those days, while science, banished by Calvin at the time of the Reformation, made a new and brilliant start. It was also during this period that the aspect of the town was enriched and beautified by elegant residences near the Treille and in the country.

The First Empire in France brought a flood of exiles and famous travellers to Geneva. Mme de Stael, at sword's points with Napoleon, established herself at Coppet and formed a circle of intellectuals and writers who have

The Lavaux countryside.

made the name of this little village near Geneva famous. The Geneva banking houses were already well-known in those days. And Voltaire's remark was much quoted: «If you see a Genevese banker jump out of a window, be sure to follow him, for there is money to be made!» Geneva has given many financiers to the world. Necker, father of Mme de Stael and financial adviser to Louis XVI, was Genevese as was Albert Galatin, who emigrated to the United States and became Secretary of the Treasury under Thomas Jefferson.

The universal spirit of Geneva has been carried forward into modern times through the work of the International Red Cross. The actual founder of the Red Cross Society was Jean Henri Dunant, who on June 14, 1859, chanced to witness the battle of Solferino and was deeply impressed by the vast amount of unnecessary suffering that resulted from the inability of the regular surgical corps to reach the thousands of wounded who lay upon the field. Three years later he published a book on his experiences, advocating an international convention to provide for the aiding of the wounded in war. This convention was held at Geneva and on August 22, 1864 a document was signed neutralizing the surgical corps of hostile armies and volunteer societies caring for the wounded. As a compliment to Switzerland, the Swiss flag in reverse colors was adopted as the emblem of the new society. Since that time Geneva has been the headquarters of the International Red Cross which has distinguished itself through its gigantic activity on behalf of suffering humanity. It is perhaps due to the fame of the Red Cross that Geneva has

Parc near Geneva

been selected as the seat of so many different international organizations : the League of Nations, whose palatial, white residence still dominates the Parc de l'Ariana, the International Labor Board, the International Board of Education, etc., etc...

The cathedral of St. Pierre, a half-Romanesque, half-Gothic structure, dominates the city. In close vicinity to the Cathedral is the ancient City Hall and opposite is the Arsenal. The city itself is divided in two by the Rhône. Seven bridges, from which fishermen can always be seen trailing their lines in the swiftly flowing water, span the river. On one bank is the popular district with its industries and crafts and on the other is the intellectual town.

When Calvin, whose spirit still hovers over Geneva, founded the University of Geneva in 1559, calling it at that time Schola Genevensis, what he had in mind was a seminary for the teaching of theology and pedagogy, although chairs of jurisprudence, mathematics, physics and astronomy were added later.

In 1892 it was declared a university with the addition of a medical faculty. At present its staff consists of 220 professors and lecturers.

Lausanne.

The quais—Wilson, Mont-Blanc, Bergues, Gustave Ador—are bordered by parks (Eaux-Vives, Grange, Mon Repos, Perle du Lac, Jardin Anglais) and in the summer the sidewalk cafes play an important role in the life of the city.

The women of Geneva are supposedly the most elegant women in Switzerland. And Gerard de Nerval once observed that although there might be lots of blue stockings in Geneva, there were also plenty of pretty legs.

The country around Geneva abounds in beautiful estates. A visit should be paid to Coppet, the home of Mme de Stael, as well as to Voltaire's home at Ferney. Genthod, until 1815 a small enclave in the Pays de Gex, is of easy access to Geneva and its lovely manors are well worth a visit. These houses retain all their beauty and freshness of 200 years ago and, in their incomparable setting, facing the lake and Mont Blanc, are a living memorial to the taste of the French refugees.

VAUD

« *Though at times his heart beats wild*
For the beautiful Pays de Vaud;
Though at times he hears in his dreams
The Ranz des Vaches of old,
And the rush of mountain streams
From glaciers clear and cold ».

From « *The Fiftieth Birthday of Agassiz*»
by Henry Wadsworth Longfellow.

The canton of Vaud—or the «Pays de Vaud» as it is called in French—
is the fourth largest Swiss canton, while its 350,000 inhabitants make it rank

A « Café » in Geneva.

Lake Leman and vineyards

third in population. It is bounded on the south by the lake of Geneva, in the west by the Jura mountains, in the east by the picturesque chain of the lower Alps and in the north by the lake of Neuchatel.

This pleasant countryside, occupied first by the Celts, then by the Romans, Alemanni, Burgundians, Dukes of Savoy, Dukes of Burgundy and finally by the Bernese, has never lost its intrinsic dignity and sense of freedom.

The Vaudois, who has his own philosophers and poets of freedom—Secretan, Vinet, Bridel—is said to « carry his liberty in his soul. »

In the great epoch of Rome, Avenches (Aventicum) was the capital of Helvetian Gaul.

It was here that the roads from Italy over the Great Saint-Bernard and from Germany through Vindonissa joined. The walls and towers of this ancient capital still stand in part today. A golden bust of the Emperor Marcus Aurelius, discovered by archeologists, can be seen in the local museum. In Orbe, which was once a colony of wealthy, retired Romans, in Yverdon, in Nyon and in Vidy below Lausanne, the Romans have left us lovely mosaics and other vestiges of their civilisation.

In the 16th century, the Bernese took possession of the country which, up until the French Revolution, paid them taxes and provided them with corn and wine. In 1723, an attempt by the heroic Major Davel to rid the land of the Bernese yoke failed before the first shot was fired. But seventy-five years later, influenced by the ideas of the French Revolution, the patriots chased the Bernese out of the country. And in 1803, Vaud became the fourteenth Swiss canton.

However, having so many different masters did nothing to change the character of the Vaudois. Rather it seems to have sharpened his natural malice and to have given him a deep sense of the relativity of all things. His slogan has always been «There is plenty of time!» When it rains, he looks forward to good weather. But when the sun shines, he expects it to rain shortly.

The Vaudois is happy-go-lucky by nature. And the story is told of three men, one from Geneva, one from Berne and one from Vaud, who went

Pestalozzi in Yverdon.

looking for snails. The shrewd Genevese brought back twenty, the man from Berne, despite the fact that the Bernese are notoriously slow, appeared with ten. But the man from Vaud showed up empty-handed. « What happened ? » asked the others. « I did catch one, » was the answer « But he got away ! »

The Vaudois is not very pleased with the Calvinistic idea of the Divinity being a jealous God. And the story is told of a peasant from Lavaux, who, visiting his ruined vineyards after a hail storm, shook his fist at the sky and exclaimed angrily :

« I won't name Anyone, but this is disgusting ! »

The Vaudois respects the authorities but at the same time criticizes them freely. He likes titles : deputy, councillor, sergeant-major, and greatly esteems clergymen and teachers, but only as long as they do not interfere with the average man drinking his glass of wine. And incidentally, this drinking of a glass of wine is very important in the canton of Vaud and no ceremony of any kind is considered complete without it.

Lausanne, situated on the lower

Students and burghers in Lausanne.

slopes of Mount Jorat and crowned by its ancient cathedral, whose consecration was attended by the Emperor Rudolf of Habsburg in 1275, is the modern and flourishing capital of the canton of Vaud. This was the city where Gibbon wrote the last three volumes of his «Decline and Fall of the Roman Empire» while sitting beneath the acacia trees on his terrace, looking out at the magnificent view of Lake Leman and the Alps of Savoy. And it is Lausanne, among the cities of French Switzerland, which is the rival of Geneva.

Lausanne likes to be thought of as a city of scholars. The University of Lausanne, originally founded in 1537 as a clerical college, became a full fledged university in 1890. During the four centuries of its history many famous men have taught here—Sainte-Beuve, Mickiewicz, Melgari, Pareto, etc. Today the university possesses five faculties : Protestant theology, law, medicine, letters and sciences, and an institute of technology. The teaching staff numbers nearly two hundred professors and lecturers.

In addition to its multitude of schools and to being the home of such distinguished scientists as Louis Agassiz, who taught at Harvard University and for whom the Agassiz Museum is named, Lausanne has produced many world famous doctors. Serious, clever men, they have always had the reputation of great simplicity in dealing with their important and wealthy clientele.

And the story is told of one of them, Cesar Roux, that when he told a Duchess to take a chair in the waiting room, and she pulled herself up to her full height and said she guessed he had not caught her name, she was the Duchess So-and-So, Dr. Roux replied : «Very well, Madame! Then take two chairs!»

The streets of Lausanne wind up and down the hillside and the Place St. François is the heart of the city. One of the best of Switzerland's many fine newspapers «The Gazette de Lausanne,» is published in this town.

Along the lakeside at Ouchy which can be reached by a funicular running down from the city, are lovely parks and restaurants and one of Switzerland's finest hotels, the Beau Rivage.

Continuing along the lakeside, we come to Vevey, Montreux, Territet and the famous castle of Chillon, celebrated in Lord Byron's poem and consequently very familar to the English speaking world.

Vevey and Montreux are both famous tourist centers and offer every imaginable advantage for a satisfactory vacation. Situated on the lakeside,

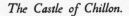

The Castle of Chillon.

protected from the northwind, with a magnificent view of the Valaisan Alps, their climate is ideal. From here many excursions can be made on mountain railways to Glion, to Les Avants, to Caux, to Rochers de Naye. While in winter, the same slopes which in spring are covered with wild narcissi, provide splendid opportunities for skiing.

One of the most popular year round resorts in this countryside is Villars, where there is a beautiful swimming pool, tennis courts and in winter, excellent skiing.

Fribourg.

FRIBOURG

« No other town has so faithfully preserved its medieval character. »
JOHN RUSKIN.

Fribourg, the eighth largest canton in Switzerland, ranks eleventh in population with 150,000 inhabitants.

The town of Fribourg, founded in 1178 by Berthold IV of Zähringen, was a Habsburg possession from 1277 to 1447, but joined the Swiss Confederation in 1481. The ancient city proper with its cathedral and Council Hall near the 500 year old lime tree is bordered on three sides by the River Saane which flows almost exactly north and south through the canton, marking fairly accurately the division between the French and German sections of the district. The old quarters are surrounded by a picturesque ring of fortifications and there are narrow, winding streets, houses with Gothic windows, fountains with Biblical subjects and steps, or steep paths, leading down to the river. Certain sections of the city date back to the days when the guilds—weavers, blacksmiths, tanners—ruled the community.

The Town Hall, built in 1522, shows the influence of the Germanic tendencies which ruled in Fribourg before Swiss mercenaries, returning from France, implanted in their native city a love of all that was French. In addition to those art treasures, typical of Fribourg, which can be seen in the museum, there are the altar screens by «le Maître à l'Œillet» and Hans Fries, as well as the altar carved by Hans Geiler in the church of the Cordeliers.

There are many schools in Fribourg, founded in the old days by eminent pedagogues like St. Canisius and Father Girard, as well as an extremely modern, bilingual, Catholic university. The University of Fribourg, which became a state institution in 1889, comprises four faculties : Catholic theology, jurisprudence, philosophy and science.

The Church of St. Nicolas with its Gothic tower, built in the first half of the 14th century, is the oldest of Fribourg's many churches and convents whose presence creates a definite mystical atmosphere which is enhanced by the unusual religious activity of this thoroughly Catholic city.

To the north of the city lies the German speaking part of the canton. Here Morat is situated, on a lake of the same name, still enclosed by the same walls as on the day when the Swiss defeated Charles the Bold before its gates. This lovely and interesting little town is well worth a visit.

In the green pastures of the Gruyère district, universally known for its cheese, the inhabitants and their customs reflect an ancient and pastoral civilization. The bearded «Armailli» is the typical Gruyère figure, with his small straw cap decorated with black velvet ribbons, his short cloth jacket with puff sleeves, his embroidered belt and salt bag. He is usually seen smoking a pipe and carrying a crooked stick. The doors of the barns are decorated with paintings of the «Armailli» leading his herd up steep mountain paths or standing in front of his chalet rallying his cattle to the tune of the famous «Ranz des Vaches» : Liauba, Liauba, poraria...

The women, in their sleeveless, blue cloth dresses, with a kerchief round their necks, white stockings, black shoes and broad flat straw hats with black velvet streamers, are famed for their courtesy. These people like to dance and eat well and their holiday meals often consist of seven different kinds of meat, spiced with sugared mustard, followed by the traditional «bagnolet» of whipped cream.

VIGNOBLES

DE LA SUISSE
OCCIDENTALE

LA CÔTE

La Côte Morges

LAUSAN

Vinzel

Luins

LAC LÉMAN

Satigny

Hermance

GENÈVE

NEUCHÂTEL

Neuchâtel

Champreveyres

Schaffiser
Cressier

Twanner

Cortaillod rouge

LAC DE BIENNE

Auvernier

LAC DU NEUCHÂTEL

Vully

Erlacher

Inser

BERNE ›

THUN ›

VAUX

Cure d' Attalens

phorin

Villeneuve

Yvorne

Aigle

VALAIS

Malvoisie

Johannisberg

Amigne

Muscat

Molignon

Fendant

Dôle

Hermitage

SION

Marc de Dôle

GASTRONOMY

CERTAINLY anyone who has ever made a trip on one of the many steamers that ply their way back and forth across the Lake of Geneva and has seen the vineyards covering the hillsides of the canton of Vaud, will not be astonished to learn that the wines of this canton are very fine and unusually popular. The vineyards between Geneva and Lausanne produce a white wine, generally known as « La Côte », while those between Lausanne and Vevey furnish a wine—also white—which goes under the general title of « Lavaux. » Of the latter, Dezaley is a particularly fine brand, while in the valley of the Rhone another very good white wine is produced, known as « Aigle. » Although it is always dangerous to generalize and particularly so when it is a question of using superlatives—still it is quite safe to say that, in a good season, the wine produced in the Lavaux region is the finest white wine produced in Switzerland.

Throughout French Switzerland trout, both broiled and « au bleu, » is a specialty. While on the shores of Lake Leman, the fish caught in that lake are served in many delicious ways in the countless attractive little restaurants to be found in every village. These fish are perch—fried or in fillets with sauce madère— fera, brochet, ombre chevalier and lotte, whose liver is a particularly tender morsel.

A favorite way of cooking the ombre chevalier is as follows : In the first place, when selecting fish, one should base one's calculations on 150 grams of fish per person. Then place some butter, a spoonful of chopped onion, and a bit of salt and pepper in a broiling pan. Lay the fish, which has been cleaned, in the pan. Add sufficient water so that the fish is half covered. Then add a wine glass of white wine and the juice of half a lemon. Cover the fish with a buttered paper and cook in a hot oven between 15-20 minutes. Serve on a hot platter with chopped parsley, slices of lemon and a white wine sauce.

Many delicious sausages and hams are produced in this part of the country, ranging from the « longeoles » in Geneva to the « boutefas, » « saucissons » and hams of Payerne.

« Croûtes aux morilles »—which is a kind of mushroom on toast—is also a very popular dish in French Switzerland. Not only is the « morille » a very popular form of mushroom throughout this countryside, but the Swiss in general pride themselves on being experts in the various kinds of mushrooms found in their woods. In season, in all the open-air markets, one sees stands heaped with piles of mushrooms, from the ordinary orange « chanterelles » to the much rarer and oddly colored varieties found in districts known only to the specialists.

In Fribourg, the cray fish which are to be found in the streams of the canton are very popular. And here, as well as in the rest of French Switzerland, frogs' legs and snails in season are a specialty. During the hunting season, be sure to try a saddle of venison or a civet de lièvre (hare) whenever you see it on the menu, for the Fribourgeois cook these two dishes particularly well.

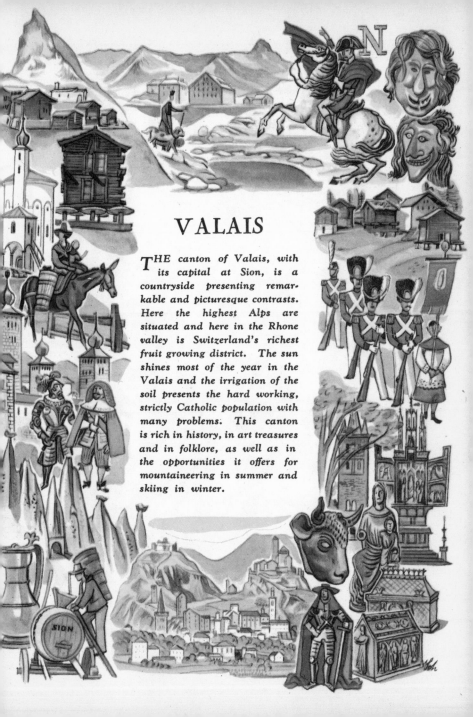

VALAIS

THE canton of Valais, with its capital at Sion, is a countryside presenting remarkable and picturesque contrasts. Here the highest Alps are situated and here in the Rhone valley is Switzerland's richest fruit growing district. The sun shines most of the year in the Valais and the irrigation of the soil presents the hard working, strictly Catholic population with many problems. This canton is rich in history, in art treasures and in folklore, as well as in the opportunities it offers for mountaineering in summer and skiing in winter.

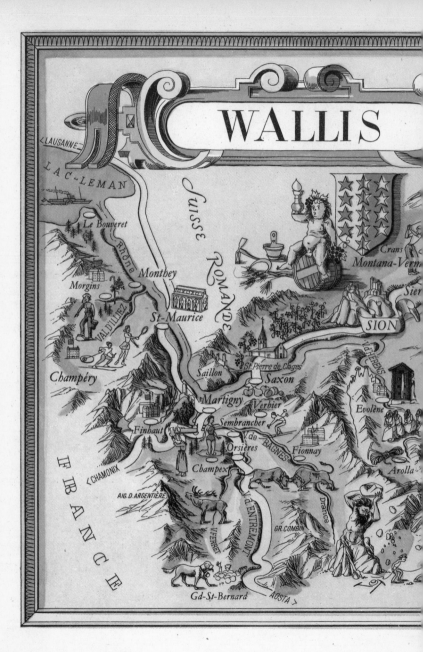

WALLIS

Lausanne

LAC-LEMAN

Rhône

Suisse Romande

Le Bouveret

Morgins

Monthey

VAL D'ILLIEZ

St-Maurice

Champéry

Saillon

St Pierre de Clages

Saxon

SION

Crans

Montana-Verm...

Sier...

V. d'HÉRENS

Evolène

Martigny

Verbier

Finhaut

Sembrancher

V. de BAGNES

Fionnay

Arolla

Orsières

CHAMONIX

Champex

AIG. D. ARGENTIÈRE

Drance

V. FERRET

V. d'ENTREMONT

GR. COMBIN

FRANCE

Gd-St-Bernard

AOSTA

The falls of Pissevache.

« *For the Valais is an incomparable country; at first I did not understand the truth of this because I compared it... with the most significant things in my memory, with Spain, with Provence (with which it is indeed, via the Rhone, related by blood) but only since I admired it for its own sake has it revealed itself in all its grandeur.*»

Rainer Maria RILKE.

E MERGING from the Lötschberg tunnel which connects Berne with Brig and passes under 6,000 feet of rock and snow, we enter the canton of Valais with the valley of the Rhone river spreading out a thousand yards below us. The Rhone itself, like a metallic snake, winds through a sandy plain lined with rows of poplars and bordered by vineyards, forests and rocky cliffs on which are perched ruined towers and castles. The colors of this countryside are gray, olive green,

Valaisan « chânes ».

yellow and red. Here are none of the vivid greens of the rest of Switzerland, but rather the same dusty, luminous landscape as in certain parts of Spain.

To the north and south, the broad, regular slopes are cover‑ed first with chestnut trees, then with meadows. Higher still is the bare, red earth with its bluish grey shadows, and, behind the first line of rocky peaks, a few snow capped summits rise against the unu‑sually light blue sky. On every level there are villages, and above the timberline, blackened chalets cluster about white Catholic churches. Some of these simple mountain chapels attain an artistic charm of a high order, as, for example, in the baroque chapel Zur Hohen Stiege, near Saas‑Fee.

These villages, with their pastures running often to the very foot of the glaciers, are located at what seem to be almost inaccessible heights. No inch of ground is lost in the Valais and the sure‑footed cattle wander in uplands which to the traveller seem unbelievably steep and remote. Many of these mountain settlements can be reached only on mule‑back over narrow trails and lie at many hours distance from the nearest center. Some of them were built by men who took refuge on the heights from the persecutions of the decaying Roman Empire. In such communities the ideas of liberty on the one hand and of neighborly co‑operation on the other have been ever present. The wooden farmsteads, particularly in the Upper Valais, are distinguished by their blockhouse‑like appearance on wooden piles, and the granaries by the circular stone slabs supporting them.

For centuries the Valaisans have lived an independent life in this separate and individualistic land of theirs. In the Middle Ages, they founded their own republic, and although they were bound to the old Swiss Confederation by traditional ties of friendship, they did not become a member until 1815. The other Swiss sometimes call them, rather contemptuously, «backward» and reproach them for being «conservatism incarnate.» It is true that the Valaisans are the most conservative and traditional minded people imaginable. And when Pope Gregory XIII, who might reasonably have expected obedience from the strictly Catholic Valaisans, introduced his new calendar, his flock on the upper Rhone refused to accept, for over 100 years, «the new fad from Rome.»

As in Corsica, bloody feuds were common in the Valais up until the late Middle Ages. Many laws from the days of the foundation of the Republic have been handed down to the present generation and the quarrels about their interpretation still go on. Sometimes lawsuits ower water rights have been drawn out over two centuries.

However, although the Valaisans are conservative, their politics somewhat turbulent and although to other Confederates they may sometimes seem «backward», in many things the Valaisans are ahead of the other Swiss. A thousand years before Karl Marx, the Valaisans organized their society on the lines of a naturally developed collectivism and their small corporations

Sion.

for mutual aid came into being long before the Swiss Confederation. Such partnerships, corporations and farmers guilds passed on the leaven for baking and allotted to each household the precious water for irrigation. Nowadays these cooperatives have made possible the use of modern machinery, such as the hydraulic wine press, which greatly decreases the labor of the vintage, yet is beyond the means of the individual wine grower.

In the alluvial plain of the Rhone, which has been put under cultivation only fairly recently, apricots, asparagus, strawberries, peaches, pears and apples are grown. On the slopes surrounding this plain there are vineyards where by grafting American vines on the local species, wine production has been increased from eight to thirty million litres annually within two decades. But unfortunately this rich, fruit growing plain is only the smallest part of the Valais, which is composed of one fifth glaciers and two fifths irrigated mountain country.

Out of the 230,000 farms in Switzerland, more than 20,000 or approximately one tenth, are in the Valais. Yet due to the glaciers and otherwise unproductive areas, not more than one thirty-third of the tillable land in Switzerland is in this canton. In other words, Valaisan properties average three times smaller than anywhere else in the country. Half of the farms are less than twelve acres in size while agricultural statistics show that twenty-five acres

The market in Sion.

A Valaisan scene.

are necessary to sustain a man and his family. The Valaisan mountain farmer lives as simply as did his primitive ancestors, eking out a difficult existence with the help of the humble wages he earns in the few large factories down in the valley. As the season changes, he also changes his place of residence, moving to his land in the high mountains in the summer months and coming down to his more temperately situated farm as winter approaches. This nomadic farming population often changes its location as much as three times during the year, following the seasons up or down the mountainsides.

There is also coal in the Valais and there is a saying that « the Rhone valley is rich in poor mines. »

In certain parts of the Valais the local spirit is so strong that people from other cantons or even from the next village are looked on with mistrust as strangers and more crimes of passion are committed in the Valais than in any other canton of Switzerland. The Valaisans are temperamental even in small matters. For instance, whenever the various village bands compete at a music festival, the rule is that each band must play the same number of  tunes. A few years ago, one band exceeded its quota, a riot took place and the offending band ended by barricading itself in a house and defiantly playing all night.

Like all people who live close to the blind forces of nature, the mountain people are very superstitious. And the Swiss writer, C. F. Ramuz, although himself a native of the canton of Vaud, in his book « La Grande Peur dans la Montagne » has painted a remarkable picture of peasant life in the high mountains in general. While in the books of the Valaisan writer, Maurice Zermatten, are to be found vivid portrayals of the life in this interesting and original canton.

There are endless festivals in the Valais and at Corpus Christi, the old uniforms worn by the eighteenth century Valaisans who fought as mercenaries in the armies of France, Spain, Austria, Prussia and Naples—and which have been carefully preserved by their descendants—may be seen.

Two languages are spoken in the Valais—French and German—and the Swiss German dialect of the Valaisans is one of the most difficult to understand among the Swiss dialects even for other Swiss. There is also, thanks to the difficulty of life in this canton, a strong tradition of emigration and today there are more citizens of Ernen in Santa Fé in the Argentine than there are in Ernen itself.

But although life is hard for the Valaisans themselves, although as a people they know what they do not want but seldom what they do, although they are far more efficient critics than improvers and although in their politics, temperament and wine play an important part, for the tourist the Valais is a real paradise.

Sion, the capital of the canton, has the beautiful church of Notre-Dame de Valère dating back to the 12th century as well as the ruins of the castle of Tourbillon perched on two neighboring hills and visible from a great distance. These two hills rising abruptly out of the surrounding plain, crowned with their lovely buildings and ruins, give an atmosphere of originality to Sion which an exploration of the town confirms. Sion has had an interesting and colorful history, dating from the time of the conquest of this countryside by the legions of Julius Caesar. In the town itself the sights which are particularly recommended are the Romanesque tower of the late Gothic Cathedral; the Supersax House with carved wooden ceilings by Jacob de Malacridis (1505) and the early baroque Council Hall with rich portico wings and the earliest Christian inscription in Switzerland, dating from the year 377 A. D. Below Sion a visit should be made to the Romanesque church of St. Pierre de Clages with its quaint octagonal spire and to the

A Valaisan « mazot ».

ruins of Castle Saillon. During the 16th century Sion, at that period the home of Matthew Schin‑ner, experienced its pe‑riod of greatest glory.

Evolène, situated at an altitude of 4140 feet, amidst forests of pines and larches in near proxi‑mity to the glaciers,—a lovely quiet spot in which to spend a vaca‑tion,—can be reached by postal autocar in an hour and a half from Sion. From Evolène it is two hours on foot to Arolla (4,700 ft) which is among even more savage and beautiful surroundings.

Sierre, where the sun shines almost all the year, is the starting point for the railway up to Montana‑Vermala where so many foreigners have regained their health. In the neighborhood of Crans Montana, there are splendid ski fields and, at Crans, one of the finest golf courses in Switzerland.

Another charming Valaisan resort is Champery, a picturesque village per‑ched on the mountainside facing the lovely Dents du Midi. Champery has a magnificent swimming pool and excellent tennis courts and it is also a center for climbing.

From Visp the road leads to Saas‑Fee, one of the most beautiful Valaisan resorts, which can be used as a center for many high Alpine excursions, including the famous « Haute Route, » over the highest mountains in the Valaisan Alps. Saas‑Fee, a small village of only 500 inhabitants, like Sierre, is another place in Switzerland where the sun usually shines. Surrounded by the highest Alpine peaks and well off the usual travel routes, it offers an ideal vacation to those travellers interested only in mountaineering or in the quiet contemplation of nature itself.

From Visp the railroad leads to Zermatt at the foot of one of the most famous mountains in the world—the Matterhorn— (14,782 ft.) which has been described as being «not a mountain but a personality.» An absolutely obligatory trip for every tourist is up the Gornergrat railway at whose terminal station there is a hotel situated facing Monte Rosa (15,217 ft.) the highest point in the Swiss Alps. Zermatt itself is an all year round resort which as far as popularity is concerned shares the honors with St. Moritz, Davos and the better known resorts of the Bernese Oberland.

At Brig, situated at the northern entrance to the Simplon tunnel, there is the picturesque Stockalper castle, built in 1642 by Kaspar Stockalper who at that time dominated the trade over the Simplon. From Brig it is not far to the Furka pass which leads to Andermatt in the canton of Uri, via the Rhone glacier, and to the Grimsel pass which leads to Interlaken in the canton of Berne.

From Brig any number of tours can be made. And one of the most interesting and rewarding is through the beautiful Lötschental where there are no automobile roads and where the population is content to cling to its ancient customs. Here, at Ferden, a festival is held on Easter Monday which is visited by the inhabitants of the other villages in the valley and where, according to an old custom, everyone receives his share of bread and cheese. The Lötschental is filled with beautiful flowers and is an ideal place for real nature lovers to spend a few days in their tour of Switzerland.

A street in a Valaisan village.

At the other end of the canton from Brig lies Martigny, a little town of seven thousand inhabitants, situated at the entrance of the Dranse and Trient valleys. Martigny is a busy and important tourist center, amidst beautiful orchards, a starting point for numerous excursions and easy ascensions. From here a railroad leads to Sembrancher, where it branches, one line leading to Orsières, where two postal bus routes start, one for the great St. Bernard, the

The sources of the Rhône.

other to the charming village of Champex. The other railroad leads to Verbier, western starting point for the «Haute Route.»

At St. Maurice stands the oldest cloister in Switzerland. The Abbey

Carrying the wine in the Valais.

church may at first disappoint the visitor Its sacristy, however, contains a world-famous collection of extremely valuable goldsmiths' work with pieces dating from the 8th century down to the present. This most ancient of all monasteries in Switzerland traces its foundation back to the Burgundian King Sigismund in 517 A. D. and

Napoléon crossing the great St. Bernard.

further to the legendary martyrs of the Christian-Roman Legion under its leader Mauritius in about 300 A.D. The foundations excavated in the monastery courtyard are characteristic witnesses of the early medieval ecclesiastical buildings of the monastery. In all, the Monastery church as it exists

today—and has existed since 1613—knew ten preceding building periods. After an inspection of the choir stalls, whose excellent workmanship dates back to about 1710, a visit should also be paid to the castle near the Rhône bridge.

The Hospice of the

A Valaisan village.

Great St. Bernard is a plain gray structure near the summit of the pass where a temple to Jupiter stood in Roman times. The hospice accomodates 300 people and the monks belong to the Order of St. Augustine. No money is asked for food and lodging. The hospitality of the monastery is still that of the olden days. In some years, as many as 30,000 travellers have been received here. And many lives have been saved by the famous St. Bernard dogs trained to rescue travellers caught in blizzards or avalanches. These dogs share, together with William Tell and the lion of Lucerne, first place in the imagination of those foreigners who have heard just a few things about Switzerland.

The chapel of the monastery, an organic part of the ancient building and containing carved choir pews from the 17th century and a tombstone to the Napoleonic General Desaix dating from 1808, is one of the highest places of worship in Europe (7616 ft. above sea level). In the main building there is a small museum and an extensive library. Special attention is due to the Late Gothic church spires with their octagonal stone cupolas and dormer windows, a type not uncommon both in the Lower Valais and on the shores of the Upper Lake of Geneva.

The Valais, like Neuchatel, is one of the least familiar cantons to the Ameri‹

can and English public. The impression exists in those countries that the highest Alps are to be found in the Bernese Oberland or in the Grisons, when it is really in the Valais that they are situated. There are twenty-eight mountains over 12.000 ft. in height in the Valais, while there are only ten in the Bernese Oberland and one in the Grisons. The history of the Valais is also little known to the English speaking world yet it is one of the most interesting of all the cantons. It is a favorite countryside for painters and writers and it was here that Rainer Maria Rilke made his home. He lies buried in the graveyard of the little church at Raron which is perched on a mountainside overlooking the valley of the Rhone. It seems only natural that writers like Rilke and Katherine Mansfield were attracted to the Valais, for there is much that is wild and strange about this countryside and much that is sad, if not tragic, too.

The Valais is one of the Swiss cantons where it is beautiful and rewarding to spend a vacation at almost every season. When the snow has melted in the regular resorts of the Grisons and the Bernese Oberland, skiing enthusiasts go to Zermatt where there is always good skiing through March and even into April. Although the Valais is the place where there are the highest mountains and consequently the mecca of all advanced mountaineers, still around every resort there are lovely walks in the larch and pine forests for those who enjoy shorter tours. And the early weeks of September are a particularly auspicious season in which to take a hiking trip through the Valais. The Valaisans themselves are as picturesque as the beautiful scenery. In Sion on Market days when the peasants come in from the surrounding countryside, it would seem as if the clock had been turned back at least a hundred years. The women with their weatherbeaten faces and their black stockings reflect the difficult life and the sturdy tradition of these mountain folk. Even the younger women who have been to the larger Swiss cities to work, when they return to their families or marry their childhood sweethearts, adopt the habits and dress of their ancestors and even in the 20th century, light colored stockings are regarded by the women of these mountain regions as a badge of sin. There are very large families in the Valais and much intermarriage. The Valaisans cling with a passionate devotion to this country of theirs and to anyone who has explored this region and fallen under its charm, this devotion is easy to understand.

The Valais is one of the cantons where the Swiss government established the work camps for the thousands of refugees who fled across the Swiss frontiers just before and all during the Second World War. Because of the critical food situation, the Swiss decided that the able bodied among these refugees should do their share in putting into effect the Wahlen plan which was calcu/lated to make Switzerland self-supporting, as far as food was concerned, by doubling the land under cultivation. Much of the new land which had to be reclaimed was situated in the Rhone valley. Here men of all nations —Belgians, Austrians, Greeks, Poles, Jugoslavs, Russians, Lithuanians and many others—cut down trees, dug out stumps and sowed crops to be turned under to enrich the sandy soil of this land. Many of these men had incre/dible adventures behind them. Many of them had wandered across the face of half of Europe before they found refuge at last in this strangely beauti/ful country. And when finally they return to their native lands they will carry in their heart the image of a land where the past and present are curiously intermingled and where their own brief residence has entered into the legends of the countryside.

GASTRONOMY

MANY famous cooks have come from the canton of the Valais, including the founder of the world-famous chain of Ritz Hotels, and in most Swiss cities there are Valaisan restaurants where the specialties of this canton are served. The Swiss like to eat well and the fact that Sion is a very popular center for assemblies and conventions is in itself a guarantee of the superiority of Valaisan cooking. Hodler, the Swiss painter, was one of the many enthusiasts for the «cuisine» of the Valais.

The Valais possesses every necessary requisite for a good wine growing country—lack of fog, little rainfall, and a summer heat that extends far into the autumn months. And as a matter of fact, the quality of the wine produced in this canton between Martigny and Brigue can hold its own with that of almost any country. Nearly 3,500 hectares of vineyard lie on the right bank of the Rhône on the southern side of the Bernese Alps. And these vineyards, with their elaborate systems of artificial irrigation, are extending further over the mountainsides each year.

The excellent climate would, however, not have sufficed alone to produce such splendid vines. The winegrowers of the Valais have given years of devoted work to removing the stones from the soil and building carefully graduated terraces so that the vines might have every protection. As far as quantity is concerned, a fairly strong white wine known as « Fendant » leads all other Valaisan wines—but it is a red wine, « Dôle, » similar to the Burgundy wines of France which takes first place in quality, not only among Valaisan wines but among all Swiss wines in general.

In the Valais are also produced several brands of the liquor, « Marc. »

Often the Valaisan winegrowers bring their tenderly nursed wines up into the high mountains for mellowing. After half a year they fetch them and sell them under the name of « Gletscherwein » (glacier wine). Other winegrowers let their grapes wither on the vines and do not pick them until Christmas. From these they press the thick sweet wine—the « flétri » wine—

such as that of Malvoisie. And the wine grown at Vispertermin and known as Heidenwein—« Pagan wine »—holds a record for being the « highest » wine in Europe, as the vineyards where it is grown lie nearly 4,000 feet above sea level.

The most popular cheese dish in the Valais is the « raclette » made from a mild cheese—by preference the « Bagnes » or the « Conches » made in the Valais itself—cut in halves and held before an open fire. As the cheese melts it is scraped off and eaten either with bread or with boiled potatoes served in the skin. This is usually followed by a plate of ham, bacon and air cured, salted meat, cut very thin.

Lamb and young goat are also very popular and well served specialties of the Valais.

The asparagus of the Valais is particularly good and is usually served with ham. In recent years, the green variety, so popular in the United States, has been introduced. But usually when you see « asperges du Valais » on the menu, it means the variety with thick, yellow, slightly bitter tasting, stalks.

Naturally, since the Valais is the most famous fruit growing district in Switzerland, dessert here usually consists of fruit. And in season, one should be sure to try both the apricots and the strawberries of the Valais—although peaches and pears, blueberries, and blackberries also grow here in great abundance and are delicious in season.

GRISONS

THE Grisons, often referred to as "Switzerland in miniature," is the largest canton in Switzerland. Here three languages—German, Italian, and Romansch—are spoken. This is the canton, together with the Bernese Oberland, which is the most familiar to the sport lovers of all nations. Here are located St. Moritz, Davos, Arosa, Flims, Lenzerheide, Klosters and many other world famous, all year round resorts. But it is not only for its sports or its beautiful mountains and 150 valleys that the Grisons is famous. It can boast as well of a rich cultural tradition and a vivid history.

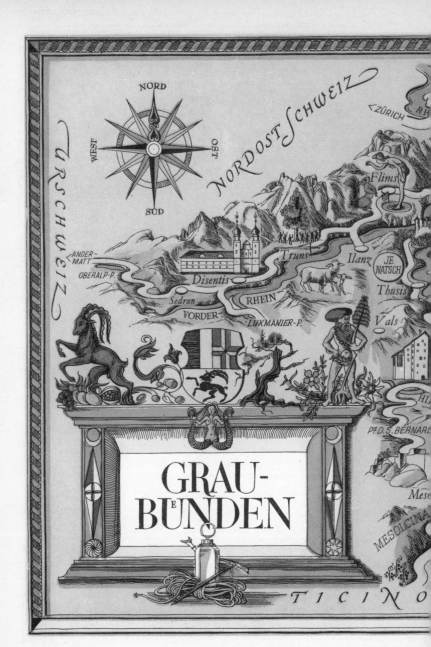

NORD

WEST
OST

SÜD

NORDOST SCHWEIZ

ZÜRICH

RH

Flims

URSCHWEIZ

ANDER-
MATT

OBERALP-P.

Disentis

Truns

Ilanz

JE
NATSCH

Thusis

Sedrun

RHEIN

Vals

VORDER-

LUKMANIER-P.

Pß D. S. BERNARD

Mese

MESOLCINA

GRAU-
BÜNDEN

TICINO

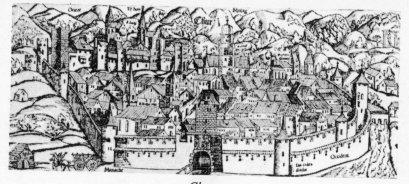

Chur.

GRISONS

« *The highways are well maintained, all people are well clothed, and everyone lives at his ease.* »
Bishop Gilbert BURNET (1643*1715).

THE canton of the Grisons is the largest canton in Switzerland, covering 2703 square miles and including more than one sixth of the Confede, ration. The canton consists of an immense network of mountains furrowed by 150 valleys and in many ways is Switzerland in miniature. Here three languages are spoken—German, Italian and Romansch. A little more than half of the population speaks German, a third Romansch and the rest, about a sixth, an Italian dialect.

Because of the mountainous nature of the country, it might be expected that this region would not have had a particularly interesting history. In reality the history of the Grisons is most dramatic. Existing records show that Rhaetus, Prince of the Etruscan tribe, first invaded this district which he named « Rhaetia, » as early as 600 B.C. In 15 B. C. this part of the country became a Roman province called Rhaetia Prima. The population fought in the Roman army and their graves have even been discovered as far distant as Libya.

The history of the Grisons actually centers around its many mountain passes which have brought great advantages but also much trouble to the canton. It was over these passes that the German emperors travelled to be crowned in Rome or to fight their enemies on Italian soil. And these passes were of such strategic importance during the Thirty Years War, that the Grisons were invaded by the armies of Austria, Spain and France. But thanks largely to the energy and ability of Jurg Jenatsch (1596·1693), a most daring and colorful individual, the country finally rid itself of foreign influence. From the 15th century onwards the « Grey Confederates » as they were called (from whence the German name of the canton : Graubünden) were on good terms with the Swiss and in 1803 their territory was incorporated in Switzerland as the 18th canton.

In addition to its mountain passes the Grisons is famous for its rivers which flow north, south and east, into the North Sea, the Adriatic and the Black Sea. The Rhine rises here—and naturally there are quarrels as to which of the contributory streams is « the » Rhine—but by the time these streams have reached Reichenau, they flow peacefully on as one river, past Chur where they are joined by the Landquart, and eventually reach the North Sea. The streams in the eastern valleys flow into the Inn which eventually joins the Danube. While the rivers to the south join the Adda and eventually flow into the Po.

It has been said that the business of the Grisons is « Germans, English, wood and cattle. » During the war years, the forests of the Grisons contributed greatly towards providing fuel to replace the coal which could no longer be imported, while the cattle of the Grisons are a sturdy small, brown race, known throughout the world. Yet cattle raising in such mountainous regions is fraught with difficulties. On account of the severity of the climate, the cattle have to be kept in stables half the year, which means large quantities of hay. Yet the farmers of the Grisons are still using the same old fashioned scythes their ancestors used. A great deal of time is also consumed driving the cattle up in the mountains to graze and then back down again into the valleys. The farmers here, as in the Valais, have a hard life which serves as a decided contrast to the fashionable cosmopolitan life led in the world famous hotels of this canton.

The people of this countryside love their homes and one need only enter an Engadiner house to be conscious of its atmosphere and the almost painful state of cleanliness which exists within. The simple but solid façade with its homely projections, its wonderful lattice and balcony always attracts the stranger. These charming gabled houses with their solid stone steps show that the people who live here spare nothing to make their houses practical and liveable. The deep windows are rich with flowers—geraniums, begonias, carnations—while flowering vines climb on the lattice work. In the winter before these same windows hang tiny bags of suet and nuts for the birds.

Medels.

These people are a proud race and the story is told of a Queen who once tried to buy a copper kettle in one of these homes. The owner was not in the least inclined to sell. When the embarrassed aide drew the owner aside and explained to him that the lady was a ruling Queen, the man never changed expression : « Very well, » he said « I will give her the kettle. But it is not for sale. » Just as these people cling to their valley dialects, in the same way they cling to their various customs and festivals. One of these in St. Moritz is the « Chalanda marz. » On the first of March, the village boys take cowbells and harness bells of all sorts and with a great noise « ring in the spring » in order to remind the Gods that the countryside still lies deep beneath the snow. The boys receive gifts in money or in kind and on the following Sunday there is a great feast for the young people and a ball for their elders. Similar festivals are the Imsuras or Alpine feasts. On these occasions all the inhabitants of the village, young and old, go on a summer day to gather the cattle who are wandering through the high mountain pastures.

Shooting and fishing are the principal pastimes of the inhabitants and the whole countryside has a rich folklore, much of which is closely related to that of Italy. In the people of the Grisons flows a strong current of religion which is not perhaps obvious to the casual eye. The Reformation found an easy entrance into these valleys where for centuries the people had had a holy and serious turn of mind. Changing destiny, especially the Thirty Years War, brought many exiles into the country and these touches of foreign blood have given a certain subtlety to the character of the people. During

the seventeenth and eighteenth centuries many of them left the country, at first only for Venice, and then later for the whole of Europe where, because they are such steady and careful workers, they made their fortunes as successful restaurant keepers and confectioners. The danger of depopulation, however, which threatens so many of the higher valleys of Switzerland is less felt in the Grisons, for here the flourishing tourist trade offers a steady employment.

The Swiss National Park, situated in the Lower Engadine, is modelled on the national parks in the United States. Here no tree can be cut, no flower plucked, no game shot. Herds of chamois climb over the rocks, roebuck graze under the larch trees and deer drink from the transparent icy streams. The capricorn, historical emblem of the Grisons, has a reserve on Piz Albris near Pontresina, while forty years ago the last bears in Switzerland were to be found in the dark forests that have since become the National Park. The capricorn of the Grisons was already famous in the 17th century. An Englishman, writing at that time, tells how the innkeeper had shown him the horns of one of these animals «by help whereof they climb up and hang on inaccessible rocks from whence the inhabitants now and then shoot at them!»

The park lies between the mountain ranges of Bernina, Ortler, Oetztaler and Silvretta and the cleft of the Ofen Pass divides it in two parts. The largest southwest group consists of the massive mountain group of the Qua, tervals and Piz d'Aint. The smaller northern part includes the Laschadu, rella, Tavru group and the Pisoc group. The highest peak is not more that 10,499 ft. but the district is very inter, esting for geologists.   Dominated by rugged mountains which with the cen, turies are decreasing in height, the valleys, filled with rocky debris, are among the wildest in the Alps. The glaciers are confined to hanging glaciers

In the Cathedral of Chur.

and the snow line lies at about 9,500 ft. The park is the richest district in the whole Alps for flowers on account of its great differences in height, its different stony foundations and its position between the east and west Alpine flower boundary. Many rare plants are to be found only here, as well as the usual Alpenroses, dwarf wild roses, Alpine grasses, shrubs and meadow flowers. In the second half of June they are at their loveliest—violets of all hues, gentian, the fiery red Leimkraut, the pure white Pyrenean ranculus, the Alpine ranculus, the golden Berghahnenfuss, the elegant grasses and sedges and of course the edelweiss.

Through all the Engadine there is an abundance of wild flowers. Hardly has the last snow melted before the meadows are carpeted with crocus and soldanella, pushing their blossoms through the snow itself. During the month of May, the valleys are covered with millions and millions of white and blue crocuses. Then comes the season of the hairy anemones in pastel shades found on the hillsides and almost before these are over, the blue gentians. In steep places, clumps of the pale rose anemone vicosa can be found as early as April. Towards the end of June when the haymaking begins the beauty of the lower meadows is somewhat spoiled, but the flowers of the high pasture land and the mountains remain beautiful through the summer with a coloring far more intense than anything seen in the lower altitudes. The canton of the Grisons protects its flowers by forbidding many of them to be dug up by the roots or picked in large quantities.

Chur (Coire), the capital of the canton, can trace its origins back to Roman days when it was known as Curia Rhaetorum. Narrow, crudely paved streets, massive stone houses and small, open squares, all bear traces of the city's history. Here the Cathedral begun in the 12th century and consecrated in 1282, is located. The interior is fascinating in the extreme. Outstanding features are the carved high altar in the choir by Jakob Russ, which dates from the end of the Middle Ages, and an almost unique collection of sacred vessels in the sacristy. Further interesting sights are the Protestant City Church, the Council Hall with its panelled room by Menhard, and the stucco work in the new and old buildings dating from 1750 and 1752 respectively. The patrician house formerly owned by the Buol Family now houses the Rhaetian Museum. The climate of Chur is extraordinarily mild. Orchards and vineyards flourish in the surrounding countryside and even figs ripen in sheltered spots.

The railroad from Chur to St. Moritz passes through Thusis, near which is located the Via Mala, one of the most magnificent gorges in the Grisons. Although the stretch of railway from Thusis to St. Moritz is only 38.34 miles long, the nature of the mountains is such that, in addition to the Albula, the longest tunnel ever built on a narrow gauge railway, there are 38 smaller tunnels passing through mountains of surpassing beauty and grandeur.

In the course of the Counter-Reformation period, many baroque churches were built in the Grisons valleys. The most important undertaking of that era was the erection of the Disentis Monastery, in the Rhine Valley, in 1685. In this countryside the traveller is also struck by the many feudal seats and castle ruins dominating the Domleschg Valley between Rhäzüns and Thusis—above all the stately Ortenstein Castle, situated on a high, rocky ter-race. In the Schams, that section of the Rhine valley above Via Mala towards Andeer, with its well-known Sgraffito House, is the church of Zillis containing the famous painted wood ceiling dating from Roman times

Another striking feature is the large number of beautifully adorned carved altars from late Gothic times in the valley churches along the Rhine and Albula river. The dwelling houses found in the upper Albula valley and the Engadine are peculiar to the district. As a protection against the cold the windows are very small and narrowed like loopholes towards the interior. The backs of the houses have high circular openings ornamentally panelled with boards and serving as haybarns and accessible through the broad front doors of the houses and the adjoining «Sulers» or roomy arched entrance halls. As elsewhere in the Grisons, here also, the high pointed dome is characteristic of the church of the late Gothic period and the octagonal cupola with a lantern turret of the baroque churches of the 17th and 18th centuries.

The Grisons.

From Samaden (5,670 ft.) there is a magnificent view of the wondrous Bernina chain : Piz Palu (12,855 ft.), Piz Morteratsch (12,317 ft.), Piz Tschierva (11,693 ft.), Piz Roseg (12,934 ft.), Piz Rosatsch (10,100 ft.) and Piz della Margna (10,376 ft.). Samaden, where one of the best golf courses in the Grisons is located, is an ideal starting point for many interesting excursions. An almost obligatory trip is to Muottas Muraigl (8,200 ft.) which is easily reached by a mountain railway and from which there is a superb view out over the lovely valley of the Inn.

The funicular goes from Muraigl station to the summit of Muottas Muraigl, the difference in height being 2,329 ft. From this summit the Maloja Pass, the watershed between the Maira which feeds the Lake of Como and the Adriatic sea, and the Inn, springing from the Longhin, and flowing into the Black Sea, can all be seen. At one side of the lake, at the entrance to the Fex Valley, lies Sils Maria, and in the centre of the valley Sils Baselgia. Nearer, in the soft green meadows, is the old Engadine village of Silvaplana, situated on the shores of the lake of the same name. The mountain panorama forms a semicircle, beginning in the south with Piz Palu and ending in the northwest with Piz Kesch. Near the white peak of the famous Piz Palu, the highest mountains in the Bernina group may be seen—Bellavista, and Piz Bernina itself above the dark masse of Piz Chalchagn. The wide ridge of Piz Tschierva and the pointed Roseg follow, and the glacier world of the Sella group, above the cleft of the Roseg valley. In the foreground one sees the massive blocks of Piz Rosatsch and Surlej, and further behind, the lovely Piz della Margna, whilst the peaks of the Bergell mountains loom over the Maloja Pass. The west side of the valley is bounded by Piz Lagrev,

House in the Engadine.

flanked by Piz Julier and Piz Albana, which in their turn give place to Piz Nair and the wild and rocky towering Piz Ot.

The valley of the Upper Engadine is a narrow, long valley lying southwest  by northeast, enclosed between parallel mountain ranges, the Bernina chain in the southeast and the Julier chain in the northwest. The length of the valley is approximately 11 miles and its average width 2 to 3 miles. There is no valley of this size and sunniness in the whole of Europe, lying at such a height above sea level. The mountains on either side ascend in gradual terraces, thus giving a better exposure to the warmth and sunshine. From Maloja (5,938 ft.), the valley floor falls away only 139 ft.

126

Andeer.

as far as the lake of St. Moritz. Owing to the height of the valley, the moutains rise only between 4,000 and 5,000 ft. This does much to avert that «shut-in» feeling that so many people experience in the valleys of the high mountains. The Upper Engadine is dotted with a series of large blue lakes—the lakes of Sils, Silvaplana, Campfèr, St. Moritz and Statz. On the mountain slopes woods of spruce and larch add their charm to the landscape. The higher, lightly wooded slopes, reach a height of approximately 7,500 ft. which is higher than anywhere else in the Alps. And between here and the line of eternal snow lie the Alpine pasture lands.

St. Moritz, undoubtedly one of the most famous resorts in the world, lies on a beautiful lake of the same name in the loftiest valley in Europe. The village of St. Moritz itself (6,089 ft.) is perched on the sunny slopes of Piz Nair (10,045 ft.). While St. Moritz Bad, whose health giving chalybeate waters were known already in Roman times, is in the valley on the lake. Although St. Moritz is now known as a centre of sport and fashion, in the

A landscape in the Grisons.

15th century it was a pilgrimage center. And the leaning tower of the old Church, which modern holiday crowds pass on their way to the famous bob run, with its hairpin curve at Sunny Corner, dates back to the year 1573.

One of the loveliest trips from St. Moritz is down to Maloja along the exquisite lakes of the Upper Engadine. This trip leads through Campfer and Silvaplana to Sils, which includes the picturesque villages of Sils Baselgia and Sils Maria. From Sils Maria a most enchanting trip can be made into the lovely Fex valley.

Maloja is situated on the summit of the lowest pass between Switzerland and Italy. This is the countryside in which Nietzsche conceived and wrote «Thus Spake Zarathustra» and from every one of the enchanting little villages which lie along the route countless excursions can be made into the mountains. From Maloja a post road leads to Chiavenna with connections to the Lake of Como and of Lugano. While from Silvaplana a post road leads over the Julier Pass to Tiefenkastel, then to Churwalden Chur. The Julier route is one of the three great Alpine passes (the Great St. Bernard, Splugen, Julier) that are known to have been used during the Roman period. Even in those days the Julier was a favorite route owing to its immunity from avalanches.

Pontresina (5,915 ft.) which can be reached from St. Moritz on the Bernina Railway via Celerina, is one of the most delightfully situated spots in the upper Engadine. The sombre pine forests which surround the village provide ideal walks for those who do not like more strenuous excursions. And from Pontresina, the Bernina Railway follows the old Bernina Post Road over the pass to Tirano, Italy, through magnificent scenic country. The Bernina railway is the highest adhesion railway in Europe, that is to say the railway which reaches the greatest height above sea level without rack and pinion. The Bernina Hospice lies at 7,398 ft. above sea level and the terminus, Tirano, at 1,360 ft. The descent from Alp Grüm to Poschiavo and further to Tirano offered great technical difficulties for the construction. Many tunnels were needed and by Brusio a complete spiral bridge had to be built. Enormous protection against avalanches and winter snows had also to be built for the depth of snow on the pass averages between 15 and 20 feet in winter. The panorama from Alp Grüm also forms a semi-circle. To the east-south-east, the first peak is the rock point of Pizzo di Sena, then comes Forcola di Rosso and further south Sassalbo. In the foreground is a view deep down to the terraces of Cavaglia and deeper still, to the blue lake of Poschiavo. In the distance, already far into Italy, are the Bergamasker Alps. Dosso di Giumello and Piz Murascio tower over the valley to the west. Further is the white peak of Pizzo di Verona connected through the elegant comb-like line of the Palü glacier with the peak of Piz Palü. This marvelous railway is kept open all the year and the trip to Alp Grüm is well worth making on a winter night when the moon is full.

The climate in the Lower Engadine is considerably warmer and the vege-tation consequently far more luxuriant. Here the ruins of ancient castles are silent reminders of the days when this part of Switzerland had to endure the yoke of Austrian tyranny.

The Flüela Pass forms the connecting link between the Lower Engadine and the Davos Valley.

Davos (5,200 ft.) was formerly known principally as a health resort. But since the opening of the railway up to Weissfluhjoch, the starting point of the famous Parsenn ski runs, Davos has become the most popular skiing center in the world. Short, very steep runs lead down to Davos itself while longer runs lead to Klosters, Küblis, Fideris and Jenaz.

Klosters, which is only twenty minutes on the train from Davos is a favorite resort for those who wish to profit from the excellent skiing in Davos and yet prefer a smaller place in which to stay. In the spring beautiful trips can be made from here up the Vereina glacier and all year round the mountains around this lovely village provide walks to suit every taste.

Arosa is another very popular resort, particularly with the Swiss themselves. And all during the winter sport season, enthusiasts may be heard arguing over the comparative merits of their favorite localities—St. Moritz, Davos, Klosters, Lenzerheide, Arosa, Flims—and each one claims that his favorite spot has the most sun and the best ski runs. But in reality it is a matter of individual taste. For no matter where you may choose to spend your vacation in the Grisons, in summer or winter, you will be sure to have a wonderful time in beautiful and healthful surroundings.

GASTRONOMY

To anyone who has visited Hansel‑mann's tea‑room in St. Moritz any afternoon between four and six when the counters are laden with every imaginable variety of delicious cake and pastry, it will not seem strange that the pastry cooks of the Grisons are known throughout the world.

Among the larger cakes which are specialties of the Grisons are the « pitta » and the « Churer Kuchen, » the « Tuorta da Nusch Engiadi‑naisa » and « Birnbrot, » the recipe for which is handed down in families from one generation to the next.

« Birnbrot » is made from pears, washed and cut into fine pieces, to which hazel‑nuts, almonds, sultanna raisins, and seasonings—cloves, cinnamon, and nutmeg—have been added. All these ingredients are mixed into a paste which somewhat resembles the filling of American mince pies and is then baked in long, oval cakes made by rolling a special kind of bread‑like mixture around the paste. « Birnbrot » keeps very well and is delicious served in thin, buttered slices.

In most Swiss cities and in many hotels, travellers can get the specialties of the Grisons, particularly the tremendously popular « Bündnerfleisch, » which is a dried meat, cut in paper‑thin slices and delicious when eaten with bread or potato salads, the whole accompanied by the red «Veltliner» wine of the Grisons.

« Salsiz » sausages, which are a kind of small, flat, salami sausage, are also a Grisons specialty and very practical for picnics, while the Grisons also produces a « Leberwurst »—liver‑sausage—which, when sliced, is eaten cold. Other specialties in the sausage line are « Tiges, » « Beinwurst » and « Enga‑diner‑wurst. »

A favorite meat dish of the Grisons is made as follows : 100 grams of raw veal and 100 grams of raw pork are mixed with 50 grams of finely cut up bacon fat and two pieces of bread from which the crust has been removed and which has been soaked in milk or broth. A paste is made of 220 grams of flour, 175 grams of butter, one quarter of a glass of milk, and the yolk of an egg. This paste is then rolled out and two‑thirds of it is used to fill a pie form. The mixture of meat is then spread in the pie form, the rest of the paste is rolled very thin and used to cover the whole and the yolk of an egg is brushed over it. The pie is then baked in a fairly hot oven for about one hour and is served hot with an accompanying dish of apple sauce or other stewed fruit.

Ragouts of all kinds are very popular in the Grisons and so is « Gitzi »— young goat—and venison in season.

Then there is the « Maluns, » a dish made of flour and boiled potatoes, baked in fat and falling into small balls. Or the « Capuns, » a sort of veget‑ able soup with bread and bacon dumplings or « knolla, » made of corn meal.

The bread in the Grisons is made mostly of corn and barley and is baked in most districts by the farmers themselves. In Puschlav, for instance, the bread is baked in the form of a ring and kept on a wooden stick in some airy place for many months. Although it becomes hard as stone, notwithstand‑ ing it remains fresh.

One of the best brands of Swiss mineral water—Passugger—comes from the Grisons.

As for wines, in addition to the extremely popular and universally drunk Veltliner, there are many brands of excellent white and light red wines produc‑ ed, around Chur. One of the most delicious of the latter is the « Maienfelder. »

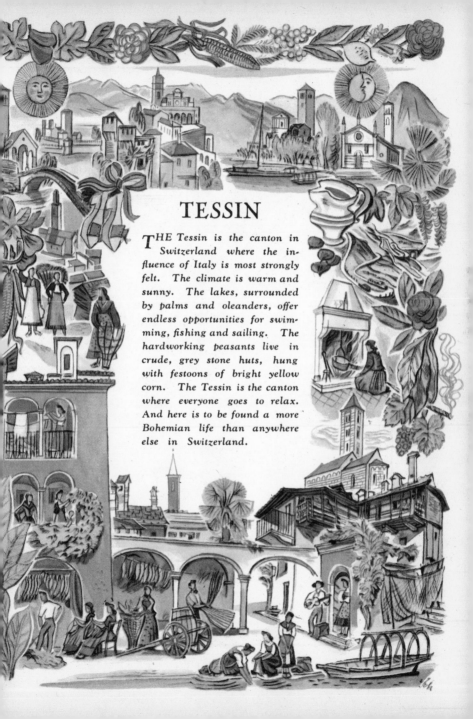

TESSIN

THE Tessin is the canton in Switzerland where the influence of Italy is most strongly felt. The climate is warm and sunny. The lakes, surrounded by palms and oleanders, offer endless opportunities for swimming, fishing and sailing. The hardworking peasants live in crude, grey stone huts, hung with festoons of bright yellow corn. The Tessin is the canton where everyone goes to relax. And here is to be found a more Bohemian life than anywhere else in Switzerland.

TICINO

GRAUBÜNDEN

ITALIA

BELLINZONA

Giubiasco

Tesserete

Gandria

LUGANO

LAGO DI LUGANO

Mᵗᵉ Generoso

Melide

Morcote

Riva San Vitale

Chiasso

Ligornetto

MILANO

Bellinzona.

« *We can only say we liked all we saw so much
that we would fain see it again and were left
with the impression that we were among the
nicest and most lovable people in the world.* »

Samuel BUTLER.

THE canton of Tessin extends from the St. Gotthard
Pass to the plain of Lombardy, an area of 1069
square miles. With the exception of three
valleys in the Grisons, it is the only place in
Switzerland where Italian is spoken. After the
dominion of the Romans who counted this
district as part of Gallia Cisalpina, the Tessin
belonged successively to the Goths, Lombards and Franks. From the beginning of the 12th century until 1403, because of its importance as a key to
the Alpine passes, it was jealously guarded by the nobles of Como and Milan
and finally monopolized by the Visconti. Then the Val Leventina went
over to Uri and Obwalden, which led to endless quarrels between the Milanese
and the Confederation. In 1798 the Tessin gained complete independence,
but only joined the Swiss Confederation permanently in 1803. The population, although predominantly of Italian origin, has been strongly influenced
by a steady migration from the cantons of inner Switzerland. This blending
of German and Italian stock has produced a race of sturdy mountain people,

courageous and independent, typically Tessiner in character, but Swiss in feeling.

Although the Alps in the Tessin are greatly inferior in height and importance of their glaciers to those of the rest of Switzerland, this canton is one of the most interesting from the point of view of art. Churches, paintings, frescos, sculptures and buildings of real merit and beauty are to be found in the most out of the way places. Tessiner artists, artisans and architects were active in all parts of Europe at the time of the Renaissance. Among the most important were Domenico Fontana, who worked on the buildings of the Vatican, Carlo Maderno, who built the façade of St. Peter's, Baldassare Longhena, the architect of the church of Santa Maria della Salute in Venice, Domenico Trezzini, one of the principal architects to draw up plans for St. Petersburg and Pietro Solari, who built part of the Kremlin.

With so much native talent, it is not surprising that the Tessin possesses gems of architectural loveliness hidden away in deep valleys. These architectural treasures combined with its incomparable scenery, go far towards making the Tessin one of the most unusual, beautiful and picturesque cantons in Switzerland.

The traveller, upon leaving Goeschenen and the wild gorges of the Reuss river, will be struck at the exit of the Gotthard tunnel by the contrast in

climate and landscape between this countryside and that of Central Switzerland. As the train slowly descends southward, the scraggy shrubs and woods
in the almost arid northern part of the canton give way to the gorgeous and
luxuriantly tropical vegetation around the lakes of Lugano and Maggiore.

Immediately upon emerging from the Gotthard is Airolo (3,756 ft.), situated
in the Leventina, the upper valley of the Tessin river. Airolo is frequented
both as a summer and skiing resort by the people of the Tessin and has the
distinction of being the birthplace of Giuseppe Motta (1871-1940), five times
President of the Confederation. It is not far from Airolo to the idyllic lake
of Ritom which can be reached by funicular and which provides the electrical
power for the Gotthard line. This lake is also famous for its trout. And
from here many lovely excursions can be made into the mountains.

The next stop of importance is Bellinzona, the capital of the canton. A
thriving administrative centre, Bellinzona is dominated by three splendid
fortresses built by the Dukes of Milan and Como as guardians of important
Alpine passes : the Gotthard, the Lukmanier and the San Bernardino. These
castles now bear the names of the three original cantons : Uri, Schwyz, Unter-

Agnuzzo on the Lake of Lugano.

walden, but formerly were known as Castello San Michele, Castello Montebello and Castello Sasso Corbaro respectively.

Although Bellinzona is a railway centre through which one usually hurries, it is well worth stopping over to visit these outstanding examples of medieval fortress architecture, as well as to walk through the crooked streets to the quaint church of La Collegiata.

One should also not fail to visit the village of Giornico, a short distance to the north of Bellinzona, which boasts of the early Christian basilica of San Nicolao. This remarkable structure is a small but beautiful example of early church architecture, with its Romanesque walls and arches, its sacrificial altar and its grotesquely carved lions.

It may well have been originally a pagan temple and is the finest and most interesting building of its kind in the Tessin.

Leaving Bellinzona, the train enters the tunnel of Monte Ceneri on its way to Lugano, which was a great commercial centre in the Middle Ages and today is one of the favorite resorts of foreigners, due to its sheltered position and fine hotels. Lugano has preserved some of its ancient character, but it is also a very modern meridional city situated on a lake and framed by wooded hills, vineyards and gardens. From the railway station high above the town, a funicular descends into the heart of the city with its open air shops, its narrow streets and arcades, reminiscent of Lombardy. Here on certain days a typical Italian market is held with a crowd of noisy, animated mer-

chants, whose goods heaped pêle-
mêle on the sidewalks in no way
detract from the charm of the scene.

Upon leaving the market and
walking out to the quayside, the
traveller is faced by a typical Riviera
picture—a promenade along the
lake, large hotels and cheery, well-
dressed crowds, come to spend their
holidays in the sun.

Lugano has a « Cercle de Culture »,
a fine museum and library, as well
as beautiful churches, such as the
Santa Maria degli Angioli, containing
admirable 16th. century frescos by
Bernardino Luini and the cathedral
of San Lorenzo, well-known for its
beautiful façade which is one of the
finest examples of early Renaissance
in the Tessin.

Excursions from Lugano should
include a trip to picturesque Gandria
with its steep, terraced vineyards.
This trip can be made either by boat
or on foot along a narrow, winding
road, overlooking the lake, or by car
on the beautiful highway which joins
Lugano to St. Moritz, passing
through Italy along the lake of Como.
For the traveller it is interesting that
Swiss postal buses, which also carry
passengers, make this trip in approximately three hours twice a day. It
is also well worth making a trip by
boat to the frontier village of Ponte-
Tresa, with a stop en route at Cam-
pione, an Italian enclave in Swiss

territory, where there is a Casino for those who wish to try their luck at the tables. Then there are ascents by mountain railways to Monte Bré, Monte San Salvatore and Monte Generoso, which afford wonderful views of the surrounding Alps. The church of Morcote, with its 360 steps, should not be missed, no more than the district of Malcantone, with its soft, undulating hills and the fertile countryside of Mendrisiotto. Of Mendrisiotto, Samuel Butler wrote : « The coup d'œil, » as a whole, is always equally striking whether one is on the plain and looks toward the mountains, or looks from the mountains to the plain. » It is only a few minutes by train from the little town of Mendrisio to the frontier village of Chiasso.

To reach Locarno, the traveller must retrace his steps to Bellinzona, where a local train takes one in twenty minutes to the town which owes its fame chiefly to the Security Pact Conference (1925) between Germany and the Allies. As one approaches the outskirts, there is a wonderful view of Lago Maggiore and the bay on which the town, enclosed on three sides by high mountains, is situated. Locarno is a quiet, restful place, with wide sunny

streets and a profusion of flowers, due to its sheltered position, which makes it a popular winter resort. Like Lugano, it also has its «Cercle de Culture» with concerts, lectures, exhibitions and its small museum, situated in the beau‹ tiful old castle, which used to be the residence of the Visconti.

It is interesting to take a walk to the quaint baroque church and through the quarter of St. Antonio, the domain of Locarno's conservative element, which is very Catholic and where the women, both young and old, always dress in deep black. High above the town, lies the pilgrim‹ age church of Madonna del Sasso founded in 1480, but several times altered and enlarged. It can easily be reached by a funicular or a steep, shady path with the stations of the cross. The church

and monastery are tended by devoted monks, who have made it into one of the loveliest pilgrimage centres of Switzerland. From its beflowered, sunny terraces, there is an incomparable view of the town and the surrounding country. The Romanesque church of San Vittore, at Muralto in the residential quarter, is also worth a visit.

Climbs above the town to Monte Bré and Orselina on sunny days are very nice half-day excursions on which to take a picnic lunch, for everywhere are sunny terraces or vine-clad pergolas from where one can enjoy the beautiful view.

Rivapiana, a hamlet about twenty-five minutes walk from Locarno along the lakeside, is reminiscent of Constantinople, with its grilled windows, behind which a veiled shadow may occasionally be glimpsed. At Rivapiana there is the mysterious «C'a di Ferro,» built in 1558 by a nobleman from Uri and serving later as barracks and prison to the Visconti.

From Locarno, it is an easy bicycle ride to Ascona, the famous and most Bohemian of Swiss resorts, which possesses a good beach and the best golf course in the canton. Originally a sleepy fishing village, it has, despite the hordes of tourists, who flock there annually, kept its typical Tessin character. It is also a favorite place of residence for artists, musicians and writers. From Ascona, it is only a step to Ronco, a charming and picturesque village perched high on the hill overlooking the beautiful road leading to Brissago, the frontier town, famous for its cigars. This same road leads on to Stresa, Italy, from where one can easily visit the lovely islands, Isola Bella and Isola Madre.

The traveller will find it convenient to use Locarno as a centre for excursions into the well-known valleys, which lie like an amphitheatre back of the town. Each valley has its own special characteristics, but all of them are poor and unproductive, due not only to the sterility of the soil, but in part to the mass emigration of the younger men to England, California and Holland in search of a more grateful existence.

The Val Verzasca, a lonely and wild gorge, through which flows a turbulent

144

river of the same name, lies nearest to Bellinzona and can be toured by car, on excellent roads, which lead through austere and solitary villages, up to Sonogno (2,980 ft.) which lies at the head of the valley and is an excellent fishing centre. Most of the population have that stern, weatherbeaten look, which comes from a constant fight with the elements in this inclement and isolated region. In winter, due to the rigors of the climate, the greater part of the inhabitants are forced down into the plains.

Procession

Directly back of Locarno, the Valle Maggia, equally beautiful, but larger and more friendly than Verzasca, does not have a good road, but instead a small train which runs parallel with the river, passing through Cevio to Bignasco, which is the end of the line. From here one can easily walk the short distance to Cavergno, a village which lies between the Val Lavizzara and the Val Bavona. Though both of these valleys are in close proximity, they are totally differ-ent in their conformation.

The Valle Lavizzara leads up a steep winding motor road to Fusio (4200) one of the loveliest and highest villages in the Tessin, surrounded by lofty snow-clad peaks. Fusio is, incidentally, also famed for good fishing.

The Val Bavona affords a tre-mendous contrast to the Valle Lavizzara and is most interesting

in a geological sense. There is no motor road into the Val Bavona which must be ascended on foot, over a rocky mule path, which leads through the hamlet of Foroglio, with its gorgeous waterfall, on to San Carlo and the glacier of the Basodino. The path winds interminably through fields containing hundreds of stone blocks of every conceivable shape and size. The villages encountered en route consist of small doleful groups of stone houses, roofed with granite slate. Incongruously enough, this pre-historic wilderness is dotted with exquisite little chapels and shrines, as if to propitiate the cosmic forces of this relentless and determined region.

On the way back to Locarno, the traveller should stop at Cevio and branch off to the left into the Valle Rovana, as far as Cerentino, where the road separates into two smaller valleys : one leading to Bosco-Gurin (4.940 ft.), the only German speaking village in the Tessin, and the other to Campo (4,430 ft.) that Renaissance wonder which, the story goes, was founded by an exiled officer of the court of the Duke d'Angouleme. At the moment, these beautiful old houses, tucked away amongst these lonely hills, are in sad need of repair.

Unfortunately for the Tessin, Campo is doomed eventually to tumble down into the gorge below, having been undermined for centuries by a torrent which, geologists claim, is slowly but surely completing its work of destruction.

All of the above named villages can be visited from Locarno in a day, as can the village of Mergoscia, which lies high above the Val Verzasca. Another excursion from Locarno is to the Val Centovalli, with its romantically perched villages and dizzy heights, spanned by rustic bridges. It is the Val Centovalli which joins Locarno to Domodossola on the Simplon line. The smaller Val Onsernone is famous for its straw industry and its beautiful women.

On the way home, the traveller should, if possible, take a bus or a car from Bellinzona up the Val Blenio, stopping to visit the much frequented spa of Acquarossa. Whether he continues over the Lukmanier pass or retraces his steps and returns via the San Bernardino is unimportant, as both are equally beautiful.

The Lake of Lugano.

An old fireplace in the Tessin.

And now, before taking leave of the Tessin, it would only be fair to pay tribute to the indomitable character of its inhabitants who despite toil, hardship and poverty, retain their courage, wisdom and humor. Their character is reflected in their folk music, with its wild strains, reminiscent of sunny lakes, rushing torrents, sterile valleys, high peaks and the never ending struggle with nature combined with a love of romance, of life and of liberty.

MALCANTONE

BELLINZONA

LID

Agno

DI MUZZANO

LU

Parad

Ponte Tresa

SAN SALVATORE

VARESE

N

Carona

Figino

Melide

Bissone

Morcote

LAGO DI LUGANO

ITALIA

Capolago

GASTRONOMY

TESSIN cooking is done chiefly with olive oil and plenty of condiments, such as garlic, onion, and aromatic herbs. The cooking in general is similar to that of Piedmont, and the people of the Tessin are very particular about the quality of their food, and consequently see to it that they have it fresh from the market each day.

All during the summer months the shops of the Tessin are heaped high with fresh vegetables and delicious fruits and berries of every imaginable variety. Dishes such as polenta, rice, and spaghetti are served in the same way as in Italy. Spaghetti is preferred « al dente » (slightly undercooked), and is served with melted butter and grated parmesan cheese—and is a staple of the diet in all classes of the population.

Minestrone soup, which is a cantonal specialty, is made in endless different varieties, according to the taste of the cook and the vegetables of the season. « Umido » or « stufato » (stew) seasoned with aromatic herbs, is a very popular dish and delicious when eaten with mushrooms and polenta. Quail, in which the Tessin abounds, is also eaten with polenta. « Capretto » (young goat) is considered a great delicacy but is eaten principally during the Easter season.

The Tessiners are also very fond of veal and pork roasts, served with a thick, brown gravy, of hare cut in quarters and roasted until golden brown, and of young chickens grilled over charcoal.

Rice—« risotto »—is very popular in the Tessin. The favorite way of preparing a « risotto » is as follows : The rice is turned in melted butter for between five to seven minutes. Then finely chopped onion is added and stirred for another two to three minutes. Water or broth is then added so that the water comes twice as high in the kettle as the rice. And the whole is cooked until the water has completely evaporated. The rice is then served at once with Parmesan cheese.

The preparation of the entire dish should not require more than twenty minutes.

The lakes and rivers abound in fish ranging from the big salmon trout to the delicate speckled variety found in the mountain streams. « Pesce Persico » is a great favorite, the perch being filleted and cooked meunière. From the lake of Lugano comes the « salmerino » which resembles trout, only is longer and narrower. In the « grottos » or inns, one usually finds « pesce in carpione, » an ordinary lake fish preserved in vinegar.

There are many different kinds of sausages in the Tessin such as the « lugha-nighe nostrane, » usually made at home and the « salametti » or « cacciatori, » which are a small, salami-type of sausage, served mostly in country inns. They are very good with a « boccalino » (pitcher-shaped wine glass made out of earthenware) of « Nostrano, » the wine of the Tessin.

The big « mortadella » sausages are excellent with polenta. And in the country, the peasants produce a kind of dried lamb or goat meat which has a fine flavor, as do the « nostrano » hams from the Valle Mesolcina.

The Tessin also has excellent cheeses, such as those of « Piora » on the lake of Ritom, which are the best in the canton. A good, though strong, cheese comes from the Valle Muggia.

Desserts in the Tessin usually consist of fresh or dried fruit, cheese, or nuts.

CENTRAL SWITZERLAND

CENTRAL Switzerland, composed of the cantons of Uri, Schwyz, Unterwalden, Lucerne and Zug, is known as the cradle of the Confederation for here is located that meadow by the Lake of the Four Cantons where the representatives of Uri, Schwyz and Unterwalden met in 1291 and pledged themselves to aid each other in their struggles against their common foes. The population of these cantons is preponderantly Catholic and extremely conservative.

RAPPERSWIL

Lachen

CHUR?

WAGGITALER-
SEE

SIHL-SEE

nsiedeln

NORDOSTSCHWEIZ

OTTO M. MÜLLER

LAUSEN-P.

LINTHAL>

UR-
SCHWEIZ

DISENTIS >
OBERALP-P.

rmatt

INO

GRAUBÜNDEN

The meadow of the « Rütli ».

« *Go to the land where Tell drew freedom's bow :*
And in the patriot's country thou shalt find
A semblance't wixt the scene and his immortal mind. »

Thomas CAMPBELL.

CENTRAL Switzerland is composed of the cantons of Uri, Schwyz and Unterwalden, which are the three original cantons of the Confederation, of Lucerne, which joined the Confederation in 1332 and of Zug, which joined in 1352. Zug is the smallest of the twenty-two cantons, both in area and population.

This whole district is known as the heart of Switzerland and the cradle of the Confederation. Here lies the Gotthard around which, in modern times, Switzerland's defenses are built and which throughout the centuries has been one of the mountain passes around which Switzerland's history

has centered. Here on the lake of Uri lies the grassy meadow known as the Rütli where it has been historically proved that the verbal agreements took place between the « forest cantons » of Uri, Schwyz and Unterwalden which led to the league of August 1, 1291 against the rule of the Habsburgs and eventually to the formation of the Confederation.

In Central Switzerland the lakes are green. The mountains are green. The trees and meadows are green. There is something eternal and enduring about this color which makes it most suitable for the land where the Confederation was founded. The population is strictly Catholic and very conservative, knowing exactly what they want and behaving stubbornly about it. In every country in the world there is a district where lives a hard-headed peasant population whose character becomes a password. In Switzerland this district is Central Switzerland. And here in the mountains there is to be found a whole folklore of odd and fascinating superstitions.

Lucerne, situated at the northwest end of the lake of the same name, at the issue of the river Reuss, is one of the best known Swiss cities in the English-speaking world, and pictures of the Lion of Lucerne hang in countless American and English homes. Mark Twain was a great admirer of the Lion of Lucerne and has left us a description of how relieved he felt when he saw a lion dying in a natural setting « where lions really do die » rather than on a pedestal in a public park.

The Lion of Lucerne, erected in 1821 to the memory of 26 officers and 760 soldiers of the Swiss guard who fell defending the Tuileries on August 10, 1792, is a monument 26 feet in length chiselled in the face of a rocky cliff 60 feet in height. It forms, owing to its romantic natural surroundings, a most impressive picture. A spring flows down one side of the rock, gathering in a pool filled with lilies and water grasses at the base. In a recess occupying the center of the cliff lies the Lion pierced by a broken lance, but still protecting the Bourbon shield with his paw. Above him is the simple inscription « Helvetiorum fidei ac virtuti » together with the names of the fallen officers.

The towers of the city wall—the Musegg,—which date from the year 1385 and which are now carefully preserved, are particular landmarks of Lucerne as are the covered wooden bridges across the Reuss. The Wasserturm, to which tradition refers as a Roman lighthouse, was in reality—like the Musegg —nothing more than a part of the fortifications of the city.

History relates that a colony of monks from the Alsatian Benedictine Abbey of the Murbach founded a little monastery on the spot where the River Reuss leaves the Lake of the Four Cantons and dedicated it to Saint Leodegar. It is on this spot where the Church of St. Leodegar stands today. With its monumental stairway it is one of the most noteworthy churches in Switzerland. Its two front spires date from the Middle Ages, while the church itself was rebuilt by Jakob Khurer after the fire of 1663. The wood carvings by Niklaus Geissler on the choir pews, on the side altars and on the huge organ which date from the same period are also most effective. Quite near here is the Ritter Palace, now housing the government's offices, and possessing a beautiful

On the Lake of the Four Cantons.

Jesuit Church in Lucerne.

arcade court dating from about 1550.

There are many charming sights in the neighborhood of Lucerne which include the two pilgrim shrines of Hergiswald beyond Kriens and Werthenstein near Wolhusen. The former, which visitors prefer to approach through the wood and up the thousand steps of the stairway, is rendered particularly charming by its abundance of early baroque appointments, the latter by the arcade court and the domed late Gothic octagonal structures which flank the contemporary Renaissance portal. In Ruswil is to be found the most beautiful of all late baroque churches that grace the landscape around Lucerne. Further attractive towns are Willisau, Sempach, Sursee with its stately late Gothic Council Hall, and Beromünster with its large Romanesque cathedral, extensively altered in the baroque period and endowed with very valuable treasures. The St. Urban Monastery, rebuilt at the beginning of the 18th century and known in particular for its extremely valuable choir stalls, possesses an outstanding baroque church.

However, although Lucerne played an important role in the history of the Confederation, present day visitors are so impressed by the beauties of the lake and mountains that they usually much rather take trips than investigate the glories of the past. There

Lucerne and the Hofkirche.

are mountain railways up both the Rigi (5,900 ft.) and the Pilatus (6,995 ft.) while the Stanserhorn is another attractive excursion point easily reached from Lucerne. Stans itself is an interesting little town full of historic associations, with an imposing monument to Arnold von Winkelried, and a Renaissance church.

It was on the Rigi that Mark Twain had the strange experience which he describes so amusingly in « A Tramp Abroad » when after climbing up the Rigi to watch the sunrise, he slept the whole day through and woke up just as the sun was sinking below the horizon. He and his friend did not realize the time and consequently were very much perturbed to find the sun travelling in the wrong direction! Mark Twain has left us the best description, of Lucerne and its lake to be found in the English language : « Lucerne is a charming place. It begins at the water's edge, with a fringe of hotels and scrambles up and spreads itself over two or three sharp hills in a crowded, disorderly but picturesque way, offering to the eye a heaped-up confusion of red roofs, quaint gables, dormer windows, toothpick steeples, with here

and there a bit of ancient embattled wall bending itself over the ridges, and here and there an old square tower of heavy masonry. The lake front is walled with masonry like a pier, and has a railing to keep people from walking overboard. All day long the vehicles dash along the avenue, and nurses, children and tourists sit in the shade of the trees, or lean on the railing and watch the schools of fishes darting about in the clear water, or gaze out over the lake at the stately border of snow-hooded mountain peaks. Little pleasure steamers, black with people, are coming and going all the time; and everywhere one sees young girls and young men paddling about in fanciful row boats, or skimming along by the help of sails when there is any wind. The front rooms .of the hotels have little railed balconies, where one may take his private luncheon in calm, cool comfort and look down upon this busy and pretty scene and enjoy it without having to do any of the work connected with it. » And then Mark Twain goes on to give his version of the trade of Lucerne, which was true in his day and which certainly is still a part of the picture of the city : « The commerce of Lucerne consists mainly in gimcrackery of the souvenir sort; the shops are packed with Alpine crystals, photographs

of scenery and wooden and ivory carvings. I will not conceal the fact that miniature figures of the Lion of Lucerne are to be had in them. Millions of them. But they are libels upon him, every one of them. There is a subtle some‹ thing about the majestic

pathos of the original which the copyist cannot get. Even the sun fails to get it; both the photographer and the carver give you a dying lion and that is all. »

Mark Twain then complains some more about the gimcracks of various kinds which are for sale and even issues a tirade against cuckoo clocks. But he falls under the charm of the Lake of Lucerne just as he fell under the charm of the Lion and in reality a trip around the lake offers a very special kind of pleasure : « For some days we were content to enjoy looking at the blue lake of Lucerne and at the piled-up masses of snow mountains that border it all around —an enticing spectacle, this last, for there is a strange and fascinating beauty and charm about a majestic snow-peak with the sun blazing upon it or the moonlight softly enriching it—but finally we concluded to try a bit of excursioning around on a steamboat and a dash on foot at the Rigi. Very well, we had a delightful trip to Flüelen, on a breezy, sunny day. Everybody sat on the upper deck, on benches, under an awning; everybody talked, laughed, and exclaimed at the wonderful scenery; in truth, a trip on that lake is almost the perfection of pleasuring. The mountains were a never-ceasing marvel. Sometimes they rose straight up out of the lake, and towered aloft and

Altdorf.

overshadowed our pigmy steamer with their prodigious bulk in the most impressive way. Not snow-clad mountains, these, yet they climbed high enough toward the sky to meet the clouds and veil their foreheads in them. They were not barren and repulsive, but clothed in green, and restful and pleasant to the eye. And they were so almost straight-up-and-down, sometimes, that one could not imagine a man being able to keep his footing upon such a surface, yet there are paths and the Swiss people go up and down them every day. »

In this passage Mark Twain has captured the peculiar charm which one feels on the Lake of the Four Cantons, where the mountains rise directly out of the lake and their green forests are reflected in its surface. This is the part of Switzerland which seems like a toy country and just as Mark Twain captured its essence from below, so does he present it from above : « Counties, towns, hilly ribs and ridges, wide stretches of green meadow, great forest tracts, winding streams, a dozen blue lakes, a flock of busy steamboats—we saw all this little world in unique circumstantiality of detail—saw it just as the birds see it—and all reduced to the smallest of scales and as sharply worked out and finished as a steel engraving. The numerous toy villages, with tiny spires projecting out of them, were just as the children might have left them when done with play the day before; the forest tracts were diminished to cushions of moss ; one or two big lakes were dwarfed to ponds, the smaller ones to puddles,—though they did not look like puddles, but like blue eardrops which had fallen and lodged in slight depressions, conformable to their shapes, among the moss beds and the smooth levels of dainty green farmland; the microscopic steamboats glided along, as in a city reservoir, taking a mighty time to cover the distance between ports which seemed only a yard apart; and the isthmus which separates two lakes looked as if one might stretch out on it and lie with both elbows in the water, yet we knew invisible wagons were toiling across it and finding the distance a tedious one. This beautiful miniature world had exactly the appearance of those « relief maps » which reproduce nature precisely, with the heights and depressions and other

A scene of Central Switzerland.

details graduated to a reduced scale, and with the rocks, trees, lakes, etc., colored after nature. »

The peculiar charm of the Lake of the Four Cantons is that here, more than anywhere else in Switzerland, civilization seems to become perpendicular. In other places in the high Alps, the mountains do not rise out of the water nor does one find hotels perched at such dizzy heights. All through this district one feels in close contact with two worlds—that of nature, and that of the tourist trade and at the same time one feels a sense of history.

Engelberg, at the foot of the snow-covered Titlis (10,527 ft.) is an increasingly popular summer resort and winter sport centre. Until the beginning of the 12th century, the surroundings of Engelberg were more or less a wilderness. But at that time Baron Conrad von Seldenbüren came from the canton of Zurich to the valley seeking a spot on which to establish an ecclesiastical place of retirement from the world. When he reached the neighborhood in which Engelberg now lies, he heard distinctly several times from the mountain the song of angels. To the pious man this was a sign from heaven that he was to build here the monastery which he had planned. Thus the Monastery of Mons Angelorum, or Mount of Angels—Engelberg—was established in 1120 A. D. Easily reached from Lucerne, Engelberg is a delightful holiday center renowned for its healthy climate, its charming situation and its facilities for sports in both summer and winter.

Weggis, on the lake of Lucerne, can be reached by steamer from Lucerne in half an hour or by car in 20 minutes. From Easter until October, Weggis, with its mild climate and sheltered situation, is an ideal place for those seeking a certain amount of diversion combined with a good rest. Steamers plying constantly back and forth on the lake offer trips for every taste. On an island just outside Lucerne is the Villa Tribschen where Richard Wagner lived from 1866 till 1872 while farther down the lake is Kehrsiten with the Bürgenstock, with its fine hotels, which also is a pleasant day's excursion.

From Brunnen, another delightful summer resort at the other end of the lake, the Axenstrasse, one of the most famous examples of highway construction in the world, leads to Flüelen, passing on the way Tell's Chapel at Sisikon and Tell's Platte a little further on. It was here that William Tell is supposed to have sprung ashore from the boat in which Gessler was taking him to prison. The whole story of William Tell takes on a much more dramatic air when one sees this picturesque countryside which was its setting.

Flüelen is the last steamboat station at the southern end of the lake and from here there is the choice of returning to Lucerne or proceeding to Altdorf, the capital of the canton of Uri. The stately church should be visited and the aristocratic houses and monumental fountains are well worth inspecting. The Council Hall Square is distinguished by an old tower and the well-known monument to William Tell.

On the Klausen road, about half an hour east of Altdorf, is the picturesquely situated village of Bürglen, the traditional home of Tell, with a stone cross, short of the village, commemorating his legendary death. The chapel was erected in 1582 and adorned with paintings at a latter date.

Close by is the ivy-clad Meier-Turm fitted up as the

Zug.

cantonal museum of antiquities.

From Altdorf we may travel up to Goeschenen at the northern entrance of the Gotthard and from Goeschenen to Andermatt which is the focus for all excursions in the region of the Gotthard.

D. H. Lawrence who was one of the few writers who have ever visited Switzerland who did not like it, has left us a seething and angry account of a walking trip he took in the Gotthard region. He was one of those people who felt oppressed in the high mountains, as if the mountains might at any minute tumble down on top of him—and he projected his spleen on everything he saw. By the time he had reached Gœschenen on his trip over the Gotthard, his anger was at its height : « Gœschenen, the village at the mouth of the tunnel, is all railway sidings and haphazard villas for tourists, post cards and touts and weedy carriages; disorder and sterile chaos, high up. How should any one stay there! I went on up the pass itself. There were various parties of visitors on the roads and tracks, people from towns incongruously walking and driving. It was drawing on to evening. I climbed slowly, between the great cleft in the rock where are the big iron gates, through which the road winds, winds half-way down the narrow gully of solid, living rock, the very throat of the path where hangs a tablet in memory of many Russians killed. Emerging through the dark rocky throat of the pass I came to the upper world, the level upper world. It was evening, livid, cold. On either side spread the sort of moorland of the wide pass-head. I drew along the high road to Andermatt.

Everywhere were soldiers moving about the livid desolate waste of this upper world. I passed the barracks and the first villas for visitors. Darkness was coming on; the straggling inconclusive street of Andermatt looked as if it were some accident—houses, hotels, barracks, lodging-places tumbled at random as the caravan of civilization crossed this high, cold, arid bridge of the European world. »

And it is quite true that here in the heart of the Gotthard region there is a very strange spirit of place which affects many people much less sensitive than D. H. Lawrence who struggled with himself to spend the night in Andermatt : « But I could not. The whole place was so terribly raw and flat and accidental, as if great pieces of furniture had tumbled out of a pantechnic-on and lay discarded by the road. I hovered in the street, in the twilight, trying to make myself stay. I looked at the announcements of lodgings and boarding for visitors. It was no good. I could not go into one of these houses. So I passed on through the old, low, broad-eaved houses that cringe down to the street out into the open again. The air was fierce and savage. On one side was a moorland, level; on the other a sweep of naked hill.

I could see how wonderful it would all be, under five or six feet of winter snow, skiing and tobogganing at Christmas. But it needed the snow. In the summer there is to be seen nothing but the winter's broken detritus. »

And so Lawrence wandered on and he closes his description of his trip over the Gotthard with a comment on the sound of the mountain streams : « The rushing of Time that continues throughout eternity, this is the sound of the icy streams of Switzerland. » And here in the Gotthard region this seems to be even more true than elsewhere, for just as this district is the cradle of the Confederation, here also the traveller feels he is in the heart of the Alps from where the spirit emanates which has held so many people from so many lands in the fascination of its grip.

Returning through Flüelen and Brunnen, we come to Schwyz, the straggling capital of the canton of Schwyz, whose museum is filled with historical treasures. Here the original Deed of Confederation of 1291 is preserved among a collection of ancient battle flags.

Zug, the capital of the canton of Zug, the smallest of the Swiss cantons, lies on the lake of the same name not far from Lucerne. The ancient town of Zug, which is even now surrounded by partly intact fortifications, is a fine example of late medieval architecture. Apart from the cathedral at Berne, the main church of Zug, St. Oswald's, is considered the most beautiful late Gothic church in the German-speaking part of Switzerland. The intricate wood-carvings in the Council Hall were also created at about the same period.

Probably the most picturesque and familiar route from Lucerne to the Bernese Oberland is by the railway over the Brünig Pass to Meiringen. After passing Alpnachstad, the starting point of the Pilatus railway, the line enters the pasture lands of Obwalden with Kerns-Kägiswil as the next station. Then there is Fluehli-Ranft and the Alpine hamlet and health resort of Melchtal in the country of Nikolaus von der Flüe. Passing Sarnen, the capital of Obwalden and Sachseln, picturesquely situated on the Lake of Sarnen, the line ascends gradually. Presently the Lake of Lungern is reached and after a few minutes climb, Brünig, the highest point on the pass with a truly wonderful view. From here the line descends to Meiringen.

GASTRONOMY

IN the hotels of inner Switzerland a delicious mixture of French and Italian cooking is served, but because this countryside has been patronized so long by an international tourist trade, the «cuisine» here is really as international as in all the larger Swiss cities.

Strangely enough, although Zug is the smallest of the twenty-two Swiss cantons, it has two very popular specialties : the « Rötel, » a small fish found only in the lakes of Zug and Aegeri, and the « Kirschtorte, » a form of pastry dessert the size of an ordinary pie, sprinkled with powdered sugar and flavored with Kirsch. The « Rötel » is only available « in season » which runs from the first of November until Christmas time. During those months the « Rötel » is one of the most popular fish dishes in Switzerland. It is cooked in various ways but is usually served fried in deep butter. Another way of serving « Rötel » is to boil the fish in water to which a leek, a bunch of soup greens, an onion spiced with cloves, and a dash of vinegar or lemon has been added. The « Rötel » should not be boiled longer than five minutes in this «bouillon.» It should then be removed from the water and served with slices of lemon and a sauce of melted butter.

Switzerland is a land where soup is usually served with both lunch and dinner. And in the country districts, the peasants frequently make their evening meal from a thick, nourishing soup.

A soup which is popular in central Switzerland is made as follows : Brown a chopped-up onion and a small piece of finely chopped garlic in fat or butter, then add a tablespoon of flour. Add several cups of water slowly, add finely diced potatoes, a cup of rice, leeks and cabbage and sufficient water to cover the whole. Cook for one and a half or two hours, adding water, so that the quantity of water remains the same.

Soups made of barley are also popular in this part of the country, as well as bread soups made by soaking small pieces of bread with a thick crust in salted water and then mashing the softened bread into a paste, adding the required amount of water. This mixture should then be brought slowly to a boil while being stirred constantly, and bit by bit finely grated cheese added together with salt and pepper. After the cheese is added, the soup should not be cooked more than ten minutes.

Another favorite dish is made of chestnuts and smoked pork. The chestnuts are soaked overnight and then cooked until soft in salted water together with the smoked pork.

A universally popular supper among the peasants is made of boiled potatoes eaten in the skins with cheese, accompanied by a bottle of wine. Naturally in the farming districts of central Switzerland, cheese is very popular.

Near the lake of the Four Cantons, the different varieties of lake fish are served in the restaurants and Arth-Goldau is a place where the trout is supposed to be particularly delicious.

Lucerne makes a speciality of vol-au-vent and of a salad of fresh vegetables, including mushrooms. This salad is known as « Luzerner Allerlei. »

Central Switzerland is not a wine-growing district, but on the other hand the canton of Zug is where the most famous Swiss Kirsch is made.

BERNE
AND THE
BERNESE
OBERLAND

BERNE, with its arcades and fountains, is the capital of Switzerland and the seat of the Federal Government. It is situated in the heart of a rich farming district with the magnificent Bernese Alps as a background. The Bernese themselves are a slow and easygoing people, but supposedly somewhat clumsy, like the bears which have been the symbol of the city since its foundation.

The Bernese plateau and Alps.

« *Majestic Berne, high on her guardian steep,*
Holding a central station of command,
Might well be styled this noble body's Head. »

William WORDSWORTH.

B ERNE, the capital of Switzerland and seat of the government since 1848, is, of all important Swiss cities, the one which has most successfully pre-served its old world charm.

Built on a promontory above the River Aare, it has a magnificent view of the Bernese Alps. And even in modern times nothing mars the architectural unity of the city.

The old town is marked off by perfectly clear boundaries—the river Aare

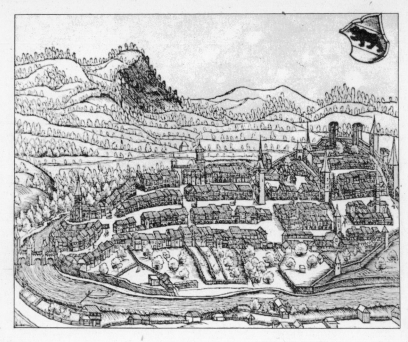

Berne.

on three sides, the line of the last walls, retained in the name of the Äusseres Bollwerk, on the fourth. Berne can be described in terms of the quaint or picturesque, but only at the cost of a radical misapprehension of her cha⸗ racter. The town was not built to be picturesque, but to fulfil a very practical function. And Berne has something far deeper than mere picturesqueness to reveal. What is unique and imposing in this city is the harmony of form and color in which the spirit of a community has incorporated itself in stone. Other towns have beautiful monuments. Berne, as it has been so aptly said, itself is a monument. The single building in Berne is astonishingly unpretentious. There are no overwhelming façades nor single beautiful houses on which endless time, thought and money were lavished. This has always been so, and travellers tales tell us how the character of Berne has withstood all the changes of time, taste and traffic. In 1479 a visitor wrote home : «Berne is a town of great wealth, and is fresh, gay, with broad streets, having vaults on either side under which one may walk with dry feet.» Another chronicler dismissed the matter more briefly. «The honest old bears,» he says «have built themselves a princely town.» In 1779, Goethe wrote to Frau von Stein : «This is the most beautiful town we have seen; the houses are built one like the other in a soft greyish sandstone.

Their equality and cleanliness do one good, especially as one feels that nothing is empty pomp or the intervention of despotism. The buildings which the state of Berne has erected for itself are great and costly, yet they have no apparatus of splendor which would make them stand out beside the others.»

Goethe had seen well when he found in the uniformity of the Bernese streets neither empty pomp nor the intervention of despotism. When in the eighteenth century a Bernese patrician tore down several of the old arcaded

On the Lake of Bienne.

A Bernese farm.

houses in the Junkerngasse to build himself a miniature palace in the French style, he created no fashion and the Erlacherhof remained isolated in Berne.

Practically the whole town was rebuilt in the early decades of the eighteenth century, but the arcades were rebuilt with it. No façade projected to break the even flight on either side of the streets, and only details—the composition of the house front with its central accent, the ornamental sculptures and iron work—show that Berne is a town of the eighteenth century.

That is what is great in Berne. It is not only that the Bernese on principle dislike useless trimmings. It would have been possible for them to have created a completely new town for they had the money—and piety towards things of the past is only a modern feeling. Moreover, as the view from the Kirchenfeld Bridge shows, they could create eighteenth century façades as well as anyone else, and the public buildings of the epoch are fully expressed in its terms. But along the streets of the old town, the expression of the individual was quite naturally absorbed in the expression of the community.

It is, perhaps, not immediately apparent to the casual eye what Berne gains from the fact

that her old streets do not run straight, but fall to the Aare in a beautiful curve. There are, however, two points from which the vital importance of this fact becomes clear. Either one must stand where the Gerechtigkeitsgasse joins the Nydeckgasse and look up the Gerechtigkeitsgasse, where the sweep of the street with its rococo balconies and red cushions is seen in all its charm; or one must cross the Nydeck Bridge and mount the Argauerstalden to the Rosengarten, where old Berne lies at one's feet. This view from the Rosengarten is the most grandiose the town has to offer. There she stands between Rathaus and cathedral—State and Church— and we can see how the town closely clothes the promontory, following exactly the contours of the terrain, so that no violence has been done to the earth. Above the ordered ranks of the saddle-roofs, the slim turrets of the cathedral suddenly pierce the air.

Situated off the European trade routes, Berne has not the commercial tradition of other Swiss cities. Whereas Basel bought her rural districts, Berne conquered hers. The Bernese were warriors and statesmen. They were never patrons of the arts. The Renaissance, humanism, romance, all passed Berne by. It was a Bernese bailiff who asked

An old street in Berne.

Voltaire, « Why in the devil do you write so much poetry? » Valerius Anshelm said of the Bernese that their virtues were manhood, the fear of God, single‑minded uprightness and ever‑watchful prudence. First the Bern‑ese had to fight. Then they had to rule. They always expelled anybody with a tendency to origin‑al thought. They had the works of Spinoza burnt and forbade the teachings of Descartes. Bishop Gilbert Burnet writing of them in 1686 describes them thus : « The men are generally sincere, but heavy... The women are generally employed in their domestic affairs and the wives, even of the chief magistrates of Bern, look into all the concerns of the house and kitchen as much as the wives of the meanest peasants. Men and women do not converse promis‑cuously together. And the women are so much amused with the manage‑ment at home and enter so little into intrigues that among them, as an eminent physician there told me, they know not what vapors are, which he imputed to the idleness and intrigues that abound elsewhere... »

This is as true today as on the day it was written, and stories about the slowness of the Bernese are proverbial. A typical one is about three peasants sitting in a café. One peasant says to another, « That cow you sold me last year is no good! » There is then a half hour's complete silence. At the end of this period, the peasant thus addressed takes his pipe out of his mouth : « It wasn't a cow. It was a calf. » Another half hour's complete silence. At the end of this second period the third peasant springs up and banging his fist vigorously upon the table cries : « If you two are going to quarrel, I'm leaving! »

Along the main street, which is called successively Spitalgasse, Marktgasse, Kramgasse and Gerechtigkeitsgasse, are a series of handsome fountains dating mostly from the 16th century. The most famous one, the Kindlifresser, shows a ferocious ogre devouring a child while several other infants are held in readiness in his pockets. Owing to the fact that the ogre wears a Jew's cap, it has been said that this fountain is a public reminder of the awful practices attributed to the Jews in olden days. Another story has it that so many children had fallen into the town moat that this figure was set up to frighten them away. Other famous fountains are the Zähringerbrunnen showing a bear fully armed with a little bear at his feet calmly eating grapes; the Samsonbrunnen, the

fountain of the guild of butchers, with whom Samson was always a favorite figure; and the Gerechtigkeitsbrunnen, the fountain of Justice, showing Justice with an upright sword moving between Emperor, Sultan, Pope and Magistrate.

The Ryfflibrunnen (Aarbergergasse, 1540/50) with its great bunch of plumes so well-known from contemporary drawings, is said to represent that Ryffli who shot Jordan of Burgistein dead through the postern of his keep after the Battle of Laupen; he represents the crossbowmen. The Dudelsackpfeifer (Spitalgasse, 1545), the fountain of the free company of minstrels, is a particularly lovely work, full of exquisite detail—the dancing children round the shaft, led by a fool in cap and bells, empty jugs, fish and dead geese, and the incomparably wistful figure of the piper himself with his goose listening entranced at his feet. The Seilerbrunnen (Käfigturm, 1549) is a portrait figure of Anna Seiler who founded Berne's great hospital. The figure is chiefly interesting for showing the graceful women's dress of the period. While the Venner Brügglerbrunnen on the Rathausplatz is remarkable rather for the energetic modelling of the shaft and capital than for the figure itself, which is a simple expression of the soldier fountain.

At the lower end of the main street is the bear-pit where the heraldic animals of the city nibble delightedly at carrots thrown them by 20th century visitors.

Bears have always been closely associated with the history of Berne. Legend has it that Berchtold of Zähringen searching for a name for the town organized a great chase in the neighborhood and vowed to call the town after the first quarry he should slay. It was a bear; so he called the town Berne.

Basel has her fearful and wonderful wildfowl, Lucerne her lion, but neither dominates the town as the bear does Berne. He lives in the flesh in the bear-pit, swaggers on the fountains or marches round their shafts, he strides across the fronts of the houses. He has even crept into

The Kleine Scheidegg.

the cathedral and sits eating grapes in the choir-stalls. It may even be said that Berne did not choose the bear but the bear chose Berne. The town became a free city in 1218. By 1224 he had pushed his way on to the town seal, never again to disappear. For a time he bore the imperial eagle nonchalantly on his back, but for centuries now he has stood there alone. He is the visible embodiment of the spirit of Berne, the outward sign of the city's inner essence. After the defeat of the French at Novarra, two bears were looted

from the French camp and brought back to Berne. They were given a home in the Käfigturm where they increased and multiplied to such an extent that in 1549 a new pit had to be built to hold the growing family. The same fate, however, befell these bears as has befallen many a noble line. Having long flourished, decadence set in. By 1798, only two or three decrepit old bears survived; and these were carried off by the French to parade in Paris. The whirligig of time had brought its revenge. A new family, instituted in 1810, died out quickly; by 1853 they were no more. In 1856, the new pit was built by the Nydeck bridge, and the family installed there was

vigorous although naturally somewhat parvenu. Eventually the population of the pits became so numerous that the shift system had to be introduced to mitigate the effects of the consistent over-feeding practised by the public. As M. D. Hottinger points out in her description of the bears of Berne, human nature is indeed a curious thing. For while the spaces of the Historisches Museum re-echo to the timorous footsteps of an occasional single visitor, and while in the Fine Arts Museum, Manuel's St. Luke contemplates his heavenly vision, untroubled by human eyes, a dense throng surrounds the bear-pits, and the

189

same man who thinks a franc a heavy sum to pay to see the Burgundian tapestries will lavish three times that amount on carrots for creatures so gross from over-feeding that at times they refuse to move and just lie inert on their backs with their mouths open, waiting for someone with a good enough aim to throw a bunch of carrots into them.

On the Kramgasse is the Clock Tower with its famous astronomical clock in whose complicated pageantry bears also play a prominent role. This clock is well worth watching as it strikes the hour of noon : «As often as the hour strikes, a troop of little bears go round in a circle, a cock crows three times before, and once after the clock strikes. A sitting man, holding a staff in one hand and an hour-glass in the other, counts the strokes by opening his mouth and smiting with his stick. Another wooden manikin rings two little bells when the hour is about to strike. In the belfry at the top of the tower are the bells and beside them stands a figure of the Duke of Zähringen in armour who strikes the hours on the bells with a hammer. »

A Bernese chalet.

Spiez.

The Cathedral of St. Vincent, begun in 1421 on plans drawn up by Matthew Ensinger, son of the great master builder of Ulm cathedral, was only completely finished in 1893. It commands a magnificent view of the city and a climb to the top of the tower is well rewarded by the splendor of the view. The portal of the Cathedral is conceived as a representation of the Last Judgment. The frescos on either side, showing the Fall and the Annunciation, are the work of Heinrich Bichler, Berne's only distinguished pre-Renaissance master. The door itself is divided into two by a pillar and each half is enframed in rich foliage. The pointed arch reuniting the halves bears fifteen brackets on which are Christ between Mary and the Baptist with the prophets on either hand. On the vaulting of the porch are the denizens of heaven and the witnesses of the Judgment, the dove of the Holy Ghost, the signs of the Four Evangelists, the Sun, Moon and Planets, the Cherubim and Seraphim, the Dominions, Principalities and Powers.

Inn on the Faulhorn.

The Rathaus, a lovely building in the late Gothic style where the Great Council of the canton of Berne meets, is also worth a visit, as are Berne's various museums.

The Swiss National Library, which contains representative volumes of the whole of Swiss literature, as well as of all literature connected with Switzerland, is also situated in Berne.

Berne University, with more than 200 professors and lecturers, is one of the largest universities in Switzerland. It was founded in 1528 as a school of theology, enlarged into an academy at the beginning of the 18th century and into a university in 1834. Today it comprises seven faculties and lectures are held in German, French, Italian and English.

Berne stands at the entrance to the

An old Inn in Grindelwald.

Bernese Oberland which is the classical region of Alpine scenery. And the farming country around Berne is among the richest in Switzerland. Furthermore it is here that the famous Emmentaler cheese is made and that we find the well-known race of Simmental cattle.

Switzerland's greatest writer, Jeremias Gotthelf, was a citizen of the canton of Berne. And in his works, the life of the Bernese peasants is vividly and richly portrayed. Born in 1797, the son of a Protestant clergyman, Gotthelf himself followed the same calling as his father until he had nearly reached the age of forty. Then he began to write the magnificent novels which are an inherent part of Swiss culture and which, from the literary point of view, compare favorably with any similar novels in world literature.

Thun, situated on the lake of the same name, at the entrance of the river Aare, is, with its quaint streets, medieval architecture, its Zähringen-Kyburg castle, and its museum in the Schadau castle, a fitting portal to the Bernese Oberland. The town offers a vast variety of fascinating walks and a

Bear-hunting.

magnificent view of the Stockhorn chain with the famous Eiger, Mönch and Jungfrau in the distance. A visit may also be paid from here to the grottos of St. Beatus.

From Thun, one may proceed by rail to Spiez and to Interlaken or the same trip can be made from the lake station Scherzligen by boat on the lake of Thun.

Interlaken is the tourist centre of the Bernese Oberland and it is from here that one gets a view of the Jungfrau in all its splendor. From Interlaken mountain railways ascend in every direction. There are delightful half-day and day excursions to the Harder, the Heimwehfluh, the Schynige Platte, Mürren via Lauterbrunnen, Grindelwald, and, most famous of all, the circular tour Interlaken-Lauterbrunnen-Wengernalp-Scheidegg-Jungfraujoch-Scheidegg-Grindelwald-Interlaken.

From Interlaken a railway takes us through pleasant orchard country to Wilderswil, a delightful summer resort which is the starting point for the Schynige Platte. And Brienz, situated on the lovely lake of Brienz, is another charming place to visit.

At Lauterbrunnen there is the magnificent Staubbach waterfall and it is from this village that the Wengernalp railway starts. It is also from Lauterbrunnen that a railway takes us to Mürren (5,358 ft.).

Wengen (4,243 ft.), a prosperous village in the midst of luxuriant pastures, is a favorite summer and winter resort. And from here the railway ascends to Kleine Scheidegg from where there is a magnificent view of the three most famous peaks of the Bernese Alps—the Eiger (13,042 ft.), the Mönch (13,465 ft.) and the Jungfrau (13,670 ft.). At Scheidegg, the Jungfrau railway begins, rising from an altitude of 6,770 ft. to a height of 11,480 ft. After a scarcely perceptible climb lasting fifteen minutes, the first stop is at the Eigergletscher station at the foot of the Eiger, near the Eiger glacier. Here there is a post office and a restaurant with a terrace. This is the starting point for climbing the Eiger, the Mönch and the Jungfrau from the northern side. After another fifteen minutes comes the Eigerwand station from where there is a magnificent view of the lower peaks with the Jura, the Vosges and the Black Forest in the distance. Ten minutes further on is the Eismeer station, a masterpiece of technical skill, cut out of solid rock. From here there is a view out over the glacier with the Wetterhorn to the left, the Schreckhorn group in the centre, and the Fiescherhoerner to the right. While the outlook from the Eigerwand is on mountains of moderate height, the view from Eismeer is of a region where ice and snow reign absolute. In still another train, the final stretch of the journey is made to Jungfraujoch (11,840 ft.). This last part of the journey takes only fifteen minutes and before we know it we are in a spot where it is possible to enjoy winter sports all year round. The hotel at the Jungfraujoch, the Berghaus, is the highest in Europe, 11,430 ft. above sea level. Situated high above the Aletsch glacier, the largest glacier in the Alps and surrounded by peaks over 13,000 ft. in height, this is a splendid centre for climbs in the mountains or on the glaciers. Near here is located the meteorological institute which carries on a great variety of interesting researches and is well worth a visit.

Grindelwald is one of the pioneer winter sport resorts in the Bernese Oberland and from here innumerable excursions can be made. The country near Grindelwald provides a particularly happy combination of peaceful valley landscape and easy accessibility to the highest Alps. Another favorite resort is Meiringen where there is the Reichenbach waterfall in which, as readers of Conan Doyle will remember, Sherlock Holmes was supposed to have disappeared.

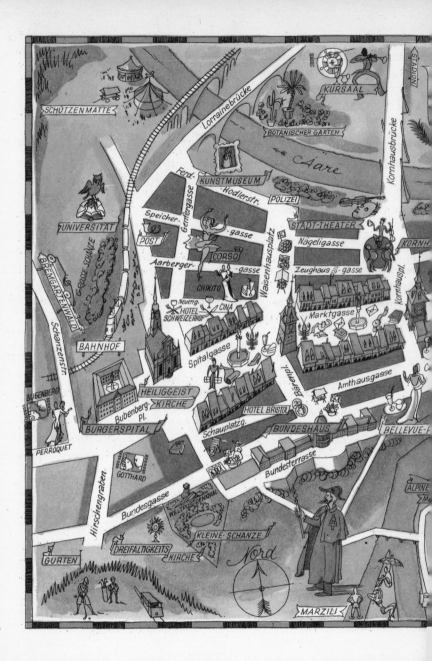

From Meiringen the railway leads via the Brünig Pass to Lucerne.

Adelboden and Kandersteg are two all year round resorts that are becoming increasingly popular, while Gstaad is a great favorite with the foreign diplomatic corps accredited to Berne.

Although the Bernese Oberland is the countryside which most closely resembles the Switzerland which has been made familiar through travel books and in literature, the beauties of the Bernese Alps are only one aspect of this canton with its wealthy farms, its picturesque chalets and its capital city from which the « honest old bears, » as the Bernese were formerly called in the olden days, rode out to conquest.

During the summer of 1946, a new Alpine highway — the Susten pass — leading from Innertkirchen in the Bernese Oberland to Wassen in Uri was opened. This technical masterpiece reaches a height of over 6500 feet above sea level.

GASTRONOMY

INN trading in the canton of Berne can look back on a long tradition. Mention of Bernese inns has appeared as early as in documents of the 14th century, but foreigners visiting the country in the 18th century mention the fact that, apart from a few specialties, meals were usually cooked « in the French style. »

Of course today in all the large hotels, both in Berne itself and throughout the countryside, an international menu is served. But if you wish to eat a dish typical of the canton, go to one of the good old inns in the country where the landlord is his own butcher and grows his own vegetables. Then ask for a « Bernerplatte. » This dish consists of bacon, sausages, ham and boiled beef, all cooked together and served with sauerkraut and potatoes. A « Berner-platte » is nothing more nor less than the festival meal of the peasants as they used to serve it at weddings, christenings, and harvest festivals—but with the years it has become one of the most popular of Swiss dishes, and is served in all the cantons throughout the country.

Two other favorite Bernese dishes are bacon, boiled with potatoes and « Lattich, » which is a form of romaine, and served as a meal in itself—and split pea soup cooked with pig's knuckles or « Gnagi. » The latter dish is prepared by cooking about 200 grams of dried yellow peas, which have been soaked overnight to soften them, in two and a half litres of water together with pig's knuckles over a slow fire. After two and a half or three hours, the pig s knuckles are removed. The soup is served with roasted bread « crou-tons » and the pig's knuckles are eaten separately with potatoes and mustard.

In the countless inns scattered throughout the Bernese countryside whose windows are picturesquely filled with geraniums, and begonias during the whole year, it is possible to obtain the usual delicious mountain trout.

Another Bernese specialty are young roosters served with roast potatoes. These young roosters are known in the Bernese dialect as « Mistkratzerli » because of their well-known habit of scratching in the manure heaps in the farm-yards.

Possibly the most popular single dish in all of Switzerland is known as

« Rösti. » This is made from potatoes first boiled, then peeled and sliced in thin slices and pressed into a cake, and browned in butter or fat until a golden brown. In Switzerland, « rösti » is the natural accompaniment of cold meats and roasts, while the peasants often make an entire meal out of it, accompanied by tomatoes or fresh green salad.

The most famous Bernese desserts are meringues served with whipped cream. And, of course, in every Bernese pastry or confectionery shop there are the Bernese « Lebkuchen »—a kind of cinnamon cake with a picture of a bear marked on them in white sugar frosting.

Naturally the most famous cheese in the canton of Berne is the Emmentaler cheese, and cheese cakes—both in the form of tarts and in larger forms, like American pies—are a Bernese specialty.

The best Bernese wines are those from the shores of the lake of Bienne, although the vineyards in the neighborhood of the lake of Thun produce very good brands, like these of «Spiez» and «Oberhofen».The «Twanner» and « Schaffiser » wines from the shores of the lake of Bienne are among the most popular and sought after white wines in Switzerland.

ZURICH

AND ITS

SURROUNDINGS

Zurich, the largest city in Switzerland, is the capital of the canton of the same name. Situated on the lake of Zurich, with the Glarner Alps in the distance, it is the most cosmopolitan of all Swiss cities and at the same time the city with the loveliest natural setting. It is an intellectual, banking and commercial center, but the spirt of Ulrich Zwingli, who preached the Reformation in the Grossmünster from 1519-1530, still hangs over the city, making it a better place in which to work than in which to play."

DEUTSCHLAND

NORD SCHWEIZ

OTTO M. MÜLLER

Schleitheim

SCHAFF

Hallau

Rhei

BASEL

Regensberg

GLATT

Bülach

LIMMAT
BASEL

KEL
LER

LAVA
TER

ZÜRICH

Affoltern

Kappel

ZÜRICH
und
NORDOSTSCHWEIZ

UR

The Falls of the Rhine.

"Zurich has always been a modern town."
M. D. HOTTINGER.

ZURICH, with a population of approximately 350,000, is the largest city in Switzerland. Situated on the lake of Zurich, with the Glarner Alps in the distance, Zurich, with its Sihl and Limmat rivers and its two ranges of low lying hills, has the most beautiful location of any Swiss city.

Its large banks, its insurance companies, its industries, its magnificent hotels and its fine shops, together with the Federal Institute of Technology and its own University, make Zurich a European, if not an international, center. But although foreigners visiting Zurich may know all the joys of a cosmo‹ politan life amidst beautiful natural surroundings, the Zurchers themselves are a very sober and hard working lot who scarcely know what the meaning

of gaiety is. Over the city hangs the spirit of Zwingli, the great Swiss Reformer, who preached the Reformation in the Grossmünster for twelve years beginning on New Year's Day in 1519. And one thing is certain : wherever the spirit of the Reformation passed, there today one finds a consciousness of sin and a tendency to take life very seriously. Zurich is a fine place in which to work, but not a very good place in which to play. For the Frauenverein, a self-righteous women's organization, sees to it that there is no weakening of that particular form of moral indignation which throughout the civilized world is regarded as the prerogative of the middle-class. When other cities of Zurich's importance are just beginning to awake and enjoy themselves, Zurich pulls down its blinds and goes to sleep. The climate of Zurich, which is inclined to be grey and foggy, also contributes to the reserved austerity of its inhabitants. Occasionally the foreigner is tempted to ask himself why these people find it worthwhile to work so hard for a life from which they seem to derive so little pleasure. But the same Puritan tradition which has always held New England in its thrall is the answer to the Zurich mentality, just as it explains much of the aloofness of the old families of

Geneva and Neuchatel. Whereas more light—minded people associate pleasure with gaiety, the Zurcher associates pleasure with work. He likes to work and consequently is really more contented than he seems. If he works hard, his conscience is quiet and after all, that is what counts.

Zurich dates back to prehistoric times when a village of lake dwellers stood near the spot where the Limmat river leaves the lake of Zurich. On the mound of the

Lindenhof, the Helvetians erected the first fortress of «Turicum» which in the year 58 B. C. fell under the power of the Romans. When the Romans finally withdrew their legions, the Alemanni became masters of the city and the Roman «Turicum» became the Alemannic «Zurich.»

Under the domination of the German Kings and Emperors the town acquired importance through the monasteries and chapters of the Fraumünster and Grossmünster, the latter of which was founded by Charlemagne and the former, in 853, by his grandson, Ludwig, who appointed his own daughter, Hildegarde, as Abbess.

The Fraumünster in Zurich.

Although historically it is not absolutely certain that Charlemagne actually resided in Zurich, legend has it that he did and the following story is told of his residence there : «It is said that here in Zurich, Charlemagne gave it to be known that he would deal justice to all, man or beast, and that any who were oppressed should ring the bell before his house, «Zum Loch,» over against the Grossmünster, while he sat at meat. One day the bell rang, but the king's servants, opening the door, saw no man and shut it again.

Then the bell rang once more and the servants, seeing no man, once more shut the door. But the king, mindful that he had promised justice to man and beast, went himself to see and there, clinging to the bell-rope, was a snake, who glided away before him and led him to her nest, where a toad sat on her eggs. Then the king ordered that the toad should be put to death, and the next day, as he sat at meal, the bell rang, and when the king's men opened, in glided the snake, passed to the king's place and dropped a precious stone into his cup. After that the good king rode away, followed by the praise and love of all the men of Zurich, and now, they say, it is he who sits on the west tower of the Grossmünster, his sword across his knees.»

«As far back as human history goes,» writes M. D. Hottinger «some kind of cult has been practised on the moraine hill on which the Grossmünster now stands. The foundation of the church itself is thus told by legend. When the cruel tyrant Decius was Governor of Turicum, there came from the west a pious Christian brother and sister, Felix and Regula, who settled by a spring of clear water on the Limmat bank, built themselves a hut and there lived a godly life, preaching the Gospel and converting many who came to hear them. But Decius had no mind to see Turicum Christian, so one day, as Felix and Regula were saying grace before their frugal dinner, he had them seized and brought before him, in order that he might compel them to abjure their Christian faith. As they steadfastly refused, he subjected them to many tortures. They were plunged into burning oil, scourged, made to drink molten lead, and all the time they were glad, and sang hymns and praised God that they might so suffer. Then Decius, seeing that no torment would avail, had them led forth and caused them to be beheaded on the banks of the Limmat where now the Wasserkirche stands, whereupon they arose and taking their heads under their arms, walked a good forty ells uphill to the holy spot where many halt and blind had been healed to the glory of God and there laid themselves down «in langwieriger Ruh,» to everlasting rest. Then a voice sounded from heaven : «Come unto Me, ye beloved of My Father and enter into the place which is prepared for you.» Later legend has associated with the two a third, Exuperantius, whose role in the matter has never been quite satisfactorily cleared up; but in any case, they stand all three on the Great Seal of Zurich, their heads in their hands.»

Tradition has it that the first Münster was the work of Charlemagne himself, who has always enjoyed great popularity in Zurich and to whom every good work has been attributed for which no other historical author existed. In any case the old wooden building was burnt down in 1078 and a new one in stone begun at once. By 1107 this new building was so far advanced that mass could be sung in the crypt. Between 1170 and 1230 the church as it stands today was built.

Zurich's history as an independent community begins in the year 1218 when Duke Berchtold V of Zähringen who had ruled over the city died childless. Then Zurich, like Berne, became an imperial city. In the great efflorescence of culture of the thirteenth century, Zurich was the center for northwest Switzerland. The beginning of the century saw the completion of her most striking architectural work—the cloister of the Grossmünster, and, at the court of the abbess, in a circle of cultured noble families, the dying Minnesang found its last refuge. Zurich even had her own Minnesänger, Hadlaub, who sang dutifully of his patron, and complained that all the nobles of the surrounding countryside could not make his lady love him.

Under the influence of Zwingli, Zurich became involved in serious quarrels with the Central Cantons. The dread of civil war hung heavy over all involved and an incident occurred as the two armies lay facing each other which is often quoted. The men of the Central Cantons had no bread and so they carried their

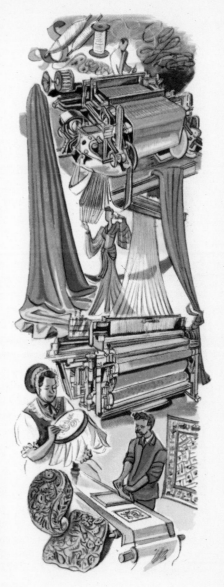

tub of milk out before the Zurich lines, crying that they had soup but no bread to break into it. Then the Zurchers came out and broke bread into the milk and ate with them, but if anyone stretched his hand over the middle of the pot, he was sharply rapped on the knuckles by a spoon of the other side and told to eat on his own land. The Burgomaster of Strasbourg, seeing this unusual sight, exclaimed, «Indeed, ye Swiss are strange folk, for, even fighting, ye are brothers.»

Hardly a township in Switzerland has fewer architectural masterpieces than Zurich. She has the Grossmünster with its cloister, one fine Renaissance fountain, the Stüssibrunnen, one remarkable Rococo guild-house, the Meise, one noteworthy dwelling-house of the same period, the Rechberg, and a few charming villas. Yet the buildings along the Limmat and in the old part of the town have a charm of their own and if one is not a strict student of architecture, Zurich seems a very attractive city.

The Federal Institute of Technology, established in Zurich in 1855, is the only institution of university standing maintained by the Federal authorities. From the very beginning it was meant to be the highest establishment in the country for technological studies and was intended to serve for teaching and research in technology and in the subjects upon which these studies are based. Great stress was laid on a close connection between lectures, practical work, laboratory work, excursions, etc., and on the adaptation of theoretical knowledge to the requirements of practical life. It has also always been the tradition of the Institute to maintain international relations and approximately 20 % of the students come from foreign countries.

Over the main entrance to the University of Zurich, is engraved the ins- cription «By the Will of the People,» for it was the people of Zurich who created the University of Zurich by public vote in 1833. A second vote in 1911 provided funds for the impressive main building with the great tower which has become the dominating feature in any view of the town. The beginnings of the University, however, go back four hundred years when Zwingli founded a school which was later called the Carolinum and which formed the backbone of intellectual life in Zurich for 300 years. The real impulse to the foundation of the present university came from the liberal movement which in Switzerland as well as throughout the rest of Europe was particularly creative at the beginning of the 19th century. Zurich owes to that movement its new constitution, its new educational system and its university. At the University of Zurich there has always been a spirit of unrestrained intellectual freedom, so much so, that certain German princes forbade their subjects to attend so notorious a home of free thought and free research. Zurich University was the first university in Europe to open its doors to women and today it is by far the largest university in Switzerland.

Zurich is the birthplace of Heinrich Pestalozzi, the great Swiss educator and it is also the city of the well-known Swiss author, Gottfried Keller. Many famous people have lived and worked in Zurich. Lenin used to study at the «Sozialarchiv» on the Predigerplatz before he was sent in a sealed train back to Russia to play a leading role in the Russian Revolution. And it was

in the Pfauen Restaurant that James Joyce, who is buried in Zurich and who was a revolutionary in the literary field, wrote many pages of «Ulysses». Joyce loved the lake and the Sihl and Limmat rivers. And one group of Zurich's citizens who always interested him were the «Securitas» men with their dogs who during Zurich's spring carnival form a protecting ring around the Bögg—a huge figure made out of cotton with firecrackers inside and burned to mark the end of winter. On less dramatic days, or rather nights, the «Securitas» act as a kind of private police to protect Zurich's better homes from prowling burglars.

Zurich's spring carnival—Sechseläuten—is one of the loveliest Swiss festivals. It is held each year on a Monday in the middle of April.

During this festival, the Bögg is burned after members of the various guilds have paraded through the streets in costume to the strains of the Sechseläuten march.

A Peasant room in Eastern Switzerland.

All evening the celebration is continued with the various guilds visiting each other and many toasts being drunk. The guilds have played an important role in the development of Zurich and the life centering around them may explain why Zurich has always been so largely a man's city.

Zurich supports a splendid stock company which plays nightly at the Schauspielhaus and an excellent opera company housed in the Stadt-theater. The city's audiences are very well known for the excellence of their critical judgment and even world famous musicians feel flatter-

The Lake of Zurich.

ed if they can wring enthusiastic applause from Zurich's expert and extremely critical musical audiences. The Cornichon cabaret is worth a visit by
anyone who understands any German at all, for here one finds Swiss wit at
its best. The artists of the Cornichon make fun of everyone and everything
both within and beyond the Swiss frontiers and for many years now the fun
has been held at a high level of excellence.

The Swiss National Museum is well worth a visit, for it has an absolutely
splendid historical collection beginning with reproductions of the villages
of the prehistoric lake dwellers and leading all through Swiss history down
to the present day. The tiled stoves here are particularly lovely as are the
Wappenscheiben, or shields of stained glass which one finds hanging in so

many Swiss homes. The Kunsthaus, at Pfauen, has the finest collection of the works of the Swiss painter, Ferdinand Hodler, whose work incorporates all the awkwardness and strength of the Swiss character, as well as the works of many other Swiss artists.

Although the history of Zurich has centered more around its rivers than around its lake, certainly today the lake is of great importance to all lovers of sports. On every fine day in the summer months its surface is dotted with sailboats, row boats, and sculls while the innumerable beaches and bathing establishments along its shores swarm with people. There are several good golf courses near Zurich and the Dolder swimming pool with its artificial waves and the indoor swimming pool, the Hallenbad, provide appropriate substitutes for those who like to swim but not in a lake. On the Zurichberg and Uetliberg, there are walks in the woods for those rare souls who still like to walk even if they can ride. And on the lake there are boats travelling constantly up and down and across for those interested in this form of excursion.

A pleasant excursion from Zurich is to Rapperswil, picturesquely situated at the upper end of the lake and reached by either boat or train. The old castle, dating from the 14th century, contains a Polish collection of treasures and relics.

From Wädenswil a line branches off to the famous pilgrimage centre of Einsiedeln with its extensive Benedictine Monastery and sacred shrines. The Abbey was founded around the year 948 on the site of the cell of St. Meinrad, who was murdered in 861. It was richly dowered with lands by the Emperors Otho II (972) and Henry II (1018) and became an independent principality of the Holy Roman Empire. The Abbey, occupying an area of 16 acres, was rebuilt in sandstone in 1704/18 and the Church, which was erected in 1719/35, is the best example of the «Vorarlberg school» in Switzerland. In the boldly constructed octagonal chamber, just inside the main entrance is the black marble Gnaden/Kapelle, rebuilt in 1817 after its destruction by the French in 1798, with the richly decked miracle working image—the Black Virgin—in wood, dating from the Gothic period.

Glarus, the capital of the canton of the same name, is situated at the foot of the Glärnisch and is within easy driving distance of Zurich. From here many pleasant excursions can be made—as for instance, to Braunwald, where each summer a popular musical festival is held. A particularly satisfying trip is over the Klausen Pass by car to central Switzerland.

Glarus is a dairying country, but there are also many industries situated here and the landscape has its own fascination although the mountains are by no means as grandiose as in the Bernese Oberland, in the Valais or in the Grisons. Glarus is one of the cantons where the Landsgemeinde is still held and the modern aspect of the town can be largely explained by the fact that it was nearly completely destroyed by fire in the spring of 1861. In Näfels stands a monument to one of the most significant battles in Swiss history.

Leaving Zurich in the other direction, we come to Schaffhausen whose name is primarily associated with the Falls of the Rhine. The Romanesque Cathedral (1101 A. D.), now a Protestant Church, is of particular interest. The old bell, cast in 1486, with the inscription, «Vivos Voco, mortuos plango, fulgura frango,» suggested to Schiller his «Song of the Bell». There is a

Arbon, on the Lake of Constance.

Inside of a Swiss Cottage.

fine museum in Schaffhausen—the All Saint's Museum—which was hit when American planes accidentally bombed Schaffhausen on April 1, 1944, but which has now been repaired. Schaffhausen, once a transhipping station for the traffic from the Lake of Constance down the river, which is here interrupted by the Falls of the Rhine, is picturesquely situated on the hilly right bank of the river. It was a free imperial town until it joined the Confederates in 1501 and is now the capital of the canton of the same name. The numerous oriel windows of the old patrician houses give an old-fashioned air to the inner city and some of its old fortifications still remain.

The Falls of the Rhine, which are the finest cascade in central Europe, do not seem particularly impressive to eyes that have seen the waterfalls of other continents, although John Ruskin did write a most flowery and enthusiastic description of them. On the same river is Stein-am-Rhein, a lovely town, which is also well worth a visit.

The whole canton of Schaffhausen gives the impression of openness and a kind of sunny charm. William Coxe in a letter from Schaffhausen wrote :

A Landsgemeinde in the Canton of Appenzell.

«I feel great delight in breathing the air of liberty; every person here has apparently the mien of content and satisfaction. The cleanliness of the homes and of the people is peculiarly striking and I can trace in all their manners, behaviour and dress some strong outlines which distinguish this happy people from neighboring nations. Perhaps it may be prejudice but I am the more pleased because their first appearance reminds me of my own countrymen and I could almost think for a moment that I am in England.» It is certainly true that the people of Schaffhausen are far less inhibited and difficult to know that most Swiss and perhaps this is just a confirmation of the argument put forward by the Swiss themselves that one of the reasons that the Swiss character is so thrown in on itself is that the country is so full of high mountains that the individual feels naturally shut in. In Schaffhausen there are

no high mountains, any more than there are in the canton of Thurgau with its rich farming and fruit growing country lying along the Lake of Constance.

Winterthur, which is known largely throughout the world because here are located the famous Sulzer Works, which make Diesel engines, is actually a city which has a remarkable cultural activity.

St. Gall, the capital of the canton of the same name, owes its name and origin to a monastery built on the site of the hermitage of Gallus, one of the early Irish missionaries, who came to these regions in about 615 A. D. This town, which grew up in the shape of a semi-circle round the convent walls, owed allegiance to the abbot until, in the beginning of the fifteenth century, its citizens made an alliance with the farmers of Appenzell and so achieved their political freedom. In the sixteenth century the Reformation, headed by the humanist Vadian, whose monument stands in the centre of the market-place, brought religious freedom as well. As a Protestant town, St. Gall formed an independent miniature state in the midst of monastic territory down to the days of the French Revolution and Napoleon, when the present canton of St. Gall was founded and the monastery was secul-arised (1803-1805). The Abbot's former palatial residence, adjoining the cathedral, is now the seat of the government and the local parliament. The Abbey church itself, rebuilt in 1756 in the Rococo style, is very imposing without and lavishly decorated within. Its magnificent painted ceiling and its wood-carving are particularly worth seeing. The cathedral library with its extreme-ly interesting world-famed collection of 30,000 volumes, its valuable manus-cripts including the plan of the abbey which dates from the 9th century is in the west wing of the Monastery. St. Gall is the oldest scholastic centre north of the Alps. Modern St. Gall possesses a number of important state schools as well as the largest private boarding school in the country. The town's university centre, the Swiss School of Economics and Public Ad-ministration of St. Gall, is, like the Federal Institute of Technology at Zurich, a centre of specialized academic studies. Apart from the schools there are numerous scientific societies and several large public libraries, a municipal theater, first class concerts and interesting museums.

A stroll over the famous «Höhenweg» is to be recommended, for the town is very much worth seeing from above. It is also a good idea to take the funicular to St. Georgen and to go on foot to «Drei Linden.» Romanshorn and Rorschach on the lake of Constance are both reached by train in 25 minutes

from St. Gall and from here during the summer months delightful excursions can be made on the lake steamers.

A delightful afternoon's excursion is to the Säntis, a mountain 8216 ft. above sea-level with a splendid view of the Alps and far out beyond the Swiss frontiers. Another greatly to be recommended excursion is into the varied countryside of the canton of Appenzell. The round trip from St. Gall, via Herisau to Appenzell and back via Gais, is one of the nicest half-day outings. Those who wish to spend a whole day in the Appenzell countryside should take the mountain railway to Wasserauen. From there it is only an hour and a half's walk to Seealpsee, one of the loveliest mountain lakes in Switzerland, 4,375 ft. above sea level.

The canton of Appenzell, which in the early days had almost no communications with the surrounding provinces has retained many ancient customs up to the present day. It is one of the cantons where the Landsgemeinde is still held, on the last Sunday in April of every year. To these assemblies the citizen of Appenzell takes great pride in carrying his sword as a token of his right to vote. The women are mostly dressed in their picturesque national costume and the youngsters consider Landsgemeinde Sunday the gala day of the year.

At Appenzell there is a procession of the cantonal officials headed by the Landammann and two state functionaries carrying halberds. All except the bailiff, who is dressed in the colors of the canton, half black and half white,

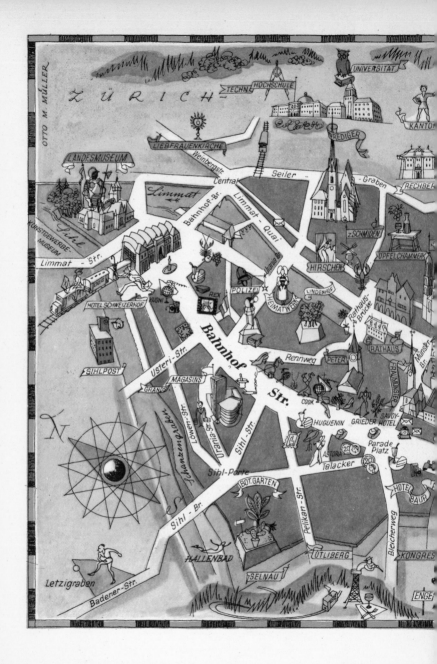

are clothed in long black gowns. On one side of the square are two platforms, the higher one accommodating the state officials and the lower one the judges of the cantonal court. The people gather in front of these platforms. With heads uncovered they stand reverently while the Landammann opens the day's proceedings with a speech, dealing with matters most important for the day. After concluding his discourse, he lays down the seal of state and descends from the platform, whereupon the cantonal secretary asks the assembly to choose a successor. The re-election or the election of a new man for each office now takes place and when the assembly is brought to a close, the people renew their oath of fidelity to the state, which in every Landsgemeinde is a most solemn and impressive act.

The whole countryside of Northeastern Switzerland presents a prosperous, fertile and well ordered picture. Here it is easy to understand why the per capita wealth of Switzerland is among the highest in the world. It is a joy to motor through this countryside and the spring season is an ideal time in which to do so, particularly when the fruit trees are in bloom. At this season the countryside around the Lake of Constance is at its loveliest and spring is also an ideal time to visit Schaffhausen, St. Gall and Appenzell. In fact, for those travellers who wish to see a bit more of Switzerland after a vacation of skiing and winter sports in the Alps, a few weeks in Zurich offer an ideal solution. For not only is it easily possible to visit St. Gall, Thurgau, Appenzell and Schaffhausen from Zurich, but even Basel is only slightly more than an hour away by train.

It has been said that although Berne is the capital of Switzerland in that it is the seat of the Federal government, it is through Zurich that Switzerland keeps pace with the modern world. Zurich's genius has always been practical and now this genius seems not only to be continuing but to be growing. All along the lake of Zurich are flourishing towns placed so near to each other that it is impossible to tell where one ends and the next one begins. And as the traveller stands on the Uetliberg, which can be climbed either on foot by wooded paths or by means of a small railway, and looks down on one side at the modern and very prosperous city around its lovely lake and then down on the other side at the wooded valley of the Sihl and further to the Alps of Central Switzerland, he is filled with wonder that such a practical and perfect compromise has been made between nature and civilization.

GASTRONOMY

THERE is no place in Switzerland where one can eat better than in Zurich. Not only is Zurich the largest city in Switzerland, but a constant stream of visitors from all parts of the world have given to the Zurich «cuisine» an international flavor. But whether the traveller dines in one of the many excellent small restaurants in the old part of the town near St. Peter's Church and along the Limmat or in the larger and more fashionable hotels, in addition to dishes of international popularity, there will always be some Zurich specialty on the menu.

One of the best known Zurich dishes is « Leberspiessli » which is made of pieces of calf's liver cut in squares and wrapped in sage leaves, then speared on thin needles of wood, alternately with pieces of bacon, the whole being cooked in a frying pan with butter and onions.

« Geschnetzeltes Kalbfleisch » is another popular Zurich dish. This is made from a good piece of veal, which has been cut up into small bits, broiled and then served with a cream or white wine sauce. This dish is eaten with « Rösti », Switzerland's national potato dish.

Often a whole meal is made from a form of stew or ragout known as « Zürcher Topf » which is made in the following manner : Two pounds of pork are cut into small pieces. To this meat is added about two pounds of sliced cabbage, a pound of diced potatoes, four or five carrots, and a finely sliced onion. All these ingredients are put into a kettle and enough hot water is added to half cover them, and the whole is cooked between one and one-half to two hours over a slow fire.

Occasionally very fine salmon trout are caught in the lake of Zurich. They are served boiled with a sauce mousseline or cold with mayonnaise and cucumber salad.

Zurich also has its own specialties in pastries, such as the « Hüppen, » —light wafers to be eaten with ice-cream—or the «Tirggel,» a type of cookie on which the coat of arms of Zurich are stamped. Zurich has also a kind of « Leckerli »—cinnamon cookies—which are very popular at Christmas time.

The cooking in Schaffhausen is similar to that in Basel and in Zurich but the fish is particularly good here—both Rhine salmon and trout.

A great Schaffhausen specialty, which is popular throughout all of Switzerland, is onion cake. This is made in the following way : Peel and cut two pounds of onions into small pieces. Turn these onions in butter or pork fat until they are glazed and brownish in color. Prepare a regular pie dough and spread in a regular pie form. Then spread the onions on the dough, and pour over them two well beaten eggs to which some cream has been added. Place in the oven and cook for about twenty minutes or until the pie crust is done.

Eight hundred and fifty hectares of the canton of Zurich are planted with vineyards. This makes Zurich the largest wine centre in the eastern part of Switzerland. The « Riesling›Sylvaner » is one of the best known Zurich wines, and other well known brands are the « Herrliberger, » « Stäfener, » and « Meilener » varieties. North of Zurich in the Schaffhausen district there are some very fine vineyards producing among other varieties the « Hallauer », « Munötler, » and « Rheinhalder » brands of wine.

HEALTH RESORTS AND SPAS

I N addition to the marvelously invigorating and curative effects of the dry, pure air of the Alps, Switzerland also possesses over 250 mineral springs whose health giving properties meet every need. Twenty-three of these springs are exploited in spas where the visitor will find excellent hotels and lovely parks together with fine walks through beautiful woods and easy journeys by the Swiss mountain railways to the higher peaks. Various sports —golf, rowing, tennis and fishing —as well as concerts and social gatherings provide pleasant relaxation without strain or nervous tension. And in these days when everyone lives at such a terrific pace, a summer vacation in one of these Swiss watering places is like visiting the fountain of youth.

Medieval baths.

Among the better known of these spas are Ragaz‹Pfae‹fers, St. Moritz and Tarasp‹Schuls‹Vulpera in eastern Switzerland and Baden, Loe‹che‹les‹Bains (Leukerbad), Schinznach and Rheinfelden in the western part of the country.

The hot medicinal springs of Ragaz‹Pfaefers, rising in the narrow gorge through which the Tamina forces its way to the Rhine, have been known for over nine hundred years. The water which rises at a temperature of 98.6 is transmitted mainly through wooden conducts over 2 1/2 miles to Ragaz and is used in 20 different treatments, includ‹ing cures for gout, rheuma‹tism, diseases of the joints, endocrine disturbances, dis‹

turbances of the circulation and high blood pressure, diseases of the veins, neuritis, neuralgia, after treatment of paralysis, intestinal troubles, diseases of the kidneys and bladder, general debility, dia‹betes and obesity.

At St. Moritz, relics of the bronze age have been discovered which prove that the mineral springs here were in use 3000 years ago. In 1537. Paracelsus, the great physician and scholar, wrote : « An acetosum

The baths of Pfäffers

A dining-room at Schinznach.

fontale, which is to be praised far above any other in Europe, is to be found in the Engadine at Sankt Mauritz ». These springs are the strongest aerated chalybeate springs in Europe and their curative power is reinforced by the beneficial influence of the magnificent climate of the Engadine. These baths are good, among other diseases, for heart trouble, disturbances of the circulation, high blood pressure, arterio-sclerosis, neuritis, sciatica, chronic arthritis and muscular rheumatism.

Tarasp-Schuls-Vulpera, where there is the only Glauber salts spring in an Alpine climate, is one of the most popular of the Swiss spas. It is beautifully situated near the Swiss National Park in the lower Engadine. Affections of the digestive organs, diseases of the liver and gall bladder, heart diseases, gout, circulatory and kidney troubles, are successfully treated here.

At Baden, near Zurich, 17 springs of the same type and temperature rise on both sides of the Limmat river. These springs were already in use in

Roman times and Baden was one of the most popular spas during the Middle Ages. Many famous writers—Poggia, Montaigne, Coryat and François le Merveilleux among others—have left us a description of spa life in olden times. Nowadays the very modern equipment at Baden provides treatment for a multitude of illnesses. And Baden is one of the Swiss spas which is open the year round.

At Loèche-les-Bains (Leukerbad) in the Valais, the calcium sulphate thermal springs reach a temperature of 123.8. This ancient spa has a long tradition of healing behind it and the guests often spend as much as five hours a day in the water, breathing in the powerful radium emanations. These baths are excellent for affections of the blood, obesity, general debility, arthritis, sciatica, thrombosis, gout and skin diseases. And the season here runs from December to March as well as from May to October.

At Schinznach, near the ancestral castle of the Habsburgs in the wide Aare valley are the strongest sulphide of hydrogen springs in Europe with a temperature of 93.2. Here there is a golf course and fine tennis courts and the whole Schinznach establishment is surrounded by lovely gardens and parks. Diseases of the bone, of the skin, and of the liver are treated here, as well as rheumatism, arthritis, diabetes and high blood pressure.

Rheinfelden, near the famous falls of the Rhine river, has brine baths as well as a drinking cure spa where all the usual diseases are treated.

Other spas are situated at Alvaneu (cold sulphur spring with calcium sulphate), Andeer (sub-thermal bitter waters containing iron and sulphates), Disentis (strongly radio-active indifferent cold spring), Fideris (aerated alkaline ferruginous spring), Teniger (calcium sulphate waters, containing sulphate of magnesium), Val Sinestra (arsenic chalybeate springs). All these spas are in eastern Switzerland, mostly in the Grisons.

In western Switzerland, in addition to Baden, Loeche-les-Bains, Schinznach and Rheinfelden, are to be found the spas of Bex-les-Bains (brine baths and mother lye), Brestenberg (simple cold spring and peat baths), Lavey-les-Bains (Thermal sulphur springs with temperature of 120.2), Lenk (cold sulphur spring, earthy chalybeate spring), Weissenburg (warm calcium sulphate spring containing magnesium sulphate, temperature 79.7), Heustrich (cold sulphur spring with high sodium carbonate content), Rietbad (radio-active sulphur spring), Vals (hot chalybeate and calcium sulphate springs in the High Alps). All these various spas have their own special charm and which one is finally selected by the traveller as the place to take a cure is a matter of individual requirements and taste.

ALPINISM

" *I have not lost the magic of long days :*
I live them, dream them still,
Still am I master of the starry ways
And freeman of the hill.
Shattered my glass ere half the sands
                                    were run
I hold the heights, I hold the heights I won. "

G. W. YOUNG.

Albrecht von Haller.

" *If I were to invent a new idolatry, I should
prostrate myself, not before beast, or ocean, or sun,
but before one of those gigantic masses to which, in
spite of all reasons, it is impossible not to attribute
some shadowy personality.* "

Sir Leslie STEPHEN.

IN ancient and medieval times, mountains were climbed for various
reasons. Philip of Macedon climbed Haemus to discover whether the
Adriatic and the Aegean could both be seen from the top. Hadrian
climbed Mt. Aetna to see the sunrise and d'Asti climbed Roche Melon
(11,605 ft.), the first high Alpine peak to be ascended, in order to found a
chapel on the summit.

The Church contributed many early mountaineers, but by far the most
distinguished of these was Father Placidus a Spescha who climbed mountains
just for the joy of climbing and who had an impressive list of conquests to

his credit. He began climbing in his late twenties and was still climbing in his seventies. And it is he who may well be called the father of mountaineering.

« Alpinism is a fine sport, » says Whymper in his « Scrambles amongst the Alps. » As a matter of fact, the Swiss do not like to hear alpinism called a sport. Football, wrestling, racing and such activities are considered sports, because they are competitions with spectators. But there is no competition in real alpinism and above all no spectators. In Switzerland, alpinism is regarded as a hobby which involves a love of nature and of the mountains themselves. The Swiss Alps have one great advantage over mount-

Crossing the Gemmi.

ains like the Caucasus and the Himalayas which may surpass them in wildness and height. The Swiss Alps are adapted to the ordinary limits of human capacity and to the period of daylight required for any well-conducted

Climbing (An old caricature).

ascent. In the Swiss Alps, the energy of the climbers is not consumed by an advance trek to their objective lasting several weeks, accompanied by a large number of carriers. Railways or motor coach services are found everywhere and there is no starting point in the

Swiss Alps which cannot be reached in a day. Naturally this constitutes a great saving in time and expense.

When a short time ago it was announced that a rope-team had « made » a record number of twelve thousand foot peaks in twenty-four hours, the announcement was received rather contemptuously in Switzerland. The Swiss are not interested in « records » in mountaineering, although there will always be certain foolhardy souls who cannot find satisfaction unless they are racing against time or risking their necks.

The whole area of the Alps is comparable to a gently inclined plane. The highest part is around Mont Blanc, near the French border. The lowest part is in the Grisons. There are twenty-eight peaks of twelve thousand feet or over in the Valais, ten in the Bernese Oberland, and one in the Grisons. Yet there are many summits below this level which are much more difficult to climb than the higher peaks. The Zermatt Breithorn is the easiest of the twelve-thousand foot peaks.

The Alps are at least fifty million years old. A tremendous pressure from the south, around Africa, is said to have shoved one layer of the earth's crust up on another, thus creating the Alps. At that time, they are supposed to have been double their present height, or in other words as much as thirty thousand feet above sea level. But the « Teeth of Time » have already gnawed half of them off. The glaciers and rivers have created deep valleys. One huge valley runs straight through the Alps from the Lake of Geneva to the Lake of Constance. Countless smaller valleys branch off from this one and through each of them flows a creek or river which, every springtime, brings down stone and slag from the Alps. The forces of nature have already been at work for millions of

The tourist at Scheidegg (An old caricature).

M. de Saussure climbing Mont Blanc.

years. But geologists estimate it will still be sixty million years before the Alps are levelled off.

The men who inaugurated what the English call the « Golden Age of Mountaineering » towards the middle of the 19th century were men of courage and vision for at that time the Alps were still surrounded with legendary perils and a tradition of inaccessibility. Mountaineering was considered in some quarters such a foolhardy sport that English climbers were often attacked in the English press, but as a famous English expert says « even the most sensitive of men can accept with Christian resignation the charge of reckless courage. » In those days mountaineering had a great attraction for intellect-uals who did not possess the qualities necessary for success in competitive sports but who had the enterprise to perceive the possibilities of mountaineer-ing and who had the necessary stamina and courage to indulge in matching their wits against the mountains. The essence of any sport is the invention of an artificial problem for the pleasure of solving it and the essence of mountaineering is the solution of the problems which the mountain provides. As Arnold Lunn points out « the true mountaineer, however much he may value the by-products of the sport such as the summit panorama, is primarily interested in the mountain as a problem to be solved. This naturally appealed to the intellectuals and it is doubtless thanks to their interest in mountaineering that there is such a vast literature in English about the Swiss mountains whereas so little has been written about the Swiss people and their way of life. »

In 1338, the Council of Lucerne jailed six clergymen for climbing Mt. Pilatus. And when two hundred years later the Mayor of St. Gall wanted to climb the same mountain out of pure curiosity, he had first to ask the permission of his colleague in Lucerne. The latter gave him not only permission to climb the mountain but a town employee to accompany him and a bottle of wine as well. This gentleman was doubtless the first mountain guide and perhaps this is when the tradition was established of the customers always providing the wine for the guides.

In 1706, a Zurich professor, J. J. Scheuchzer began to take a great interest in the Alps and together with his students often made trips through them. People were interested in hearing about his experiences. He received letters from all over the world—particularly from England. And Scheuchzer became a source of information on all Alpine questions.

Before climbing the Alps became popular, these mountains had begun to play a role in poetry and literature. Albert Haller, writing in Berne in 1729, composed a poem of four hundred and ninety verses about them. This poem became a best seller and was translated into French, English and Italian. Gradually people began to have more confidence in the Alps and to lose their old superstitious fear. Mont Blanc was a favorite subject with the painter, Conrad Witz. He had been ordered to paint an altar piece for a bishop and chose Peter's draught of the fishes which he placed on Lake Leman, with the snow-capped peak of Mont Blanc in the background. This was in 1444, the first time that an Alpine peak was immortalized by a painter.

In former days there were many quarrels about the advantages of guideless climbing and one Englishman who was a great mountaineering expert wrote : « Whilst the true mountaineer is undoubtedly the noblest work of God, a thing that is pushed and hustled up peaks by Swiss peasants and which is so wholly unable to take care of itself that it cannot be trusted to sit on a crag unroped, is as contemptible an object as may easily be imagined ».

And Ruskin, who loved Switzerland and the Alps was sometimes in despair over the effect of mountaineering on his friends :

« The real ground for reprehension of Alpine climbing is that, with less cause, it excites more vanity than any other athletic skill— while no good soldier talks of the charge he led, nor any good sailor of the helm he held, every man among the Alps seems to lose his senses and modesty with the fall of the barometer and returns from his Nephelo-coccygia brandishing his ice-axe in everybody's face. »

Saxifraga oppositifolia.

Semper vivum montanum.

In 1787, Saussure, a young natural scientist from Geneva, offered a prize to anyone who succeeded in climbing Mont Blanc. Paccard and Balmat, a doctor and a hunter from Chamonix, were the first to succeed although there is a whole library of literature on certain controversial aspects of these early ascents. Saussure's own attempt was the second successful one. Six days later an Englishman reached the top, while it was 1819 before the first American got there.

Since then the English have become outstanding Alpinists, specializing on twelve-thousand foot peaks. Whymper achieved the greatest triumph of all when he conquered the Matterhorn in 1865, a peak considered by the English unscalable up until that time. Four out of the seven men fell to their death on the descent. And Queen

Dryas octopetala.

Victoria asked her Ministers if such things should not be forbidden. The English had already founded their Alpine club in London in 1857, while the Swiss did not found theirs until 1863.

Recently « north walls » have become fashionable. The north wall of the Matterhorn was climbed in 1931 and that of the Eiger in 1938. But there are still plenty of routes and northern walls left for those who can only find satisfaction in trick climbs. In 1811, people were satisfied to have found one way to the top of the Jungfrau. Today the guide book of the Swiss Alpine Club lists twenty-one routes up the Jungfrau, while Steuri, the mountain guide from Grindelwald, celebrated, in 1940, his thousandth trip up the Jungfrau.

In Switzerland a man becomes a mountain guide not just by chance but because he lives in the mountains and loves them as did his father and grandfather before him. The guides who more than a hundred and fifty years ago carried provisions and blankets up the mountains for geologists, artists and surly lords were herdsmen, hunters and exceptionally hardy youths who knew neither fear nor giddiness. The present day guide has evolved during the course of the years from these prototypes. He now wears on his coat the badge of the Swiss Alpine Club and carries in his pocket the guide book of his cantonal government. The statut-

Gentiana clusius.

Rhododendron ferrugineum.

ory regulation of the calling of Alpine Guide was instituted about ninety years ago. During this period Swiss guides, together with their employers, completed the conquest of the Alps, and many an ice-axe from the Lütschinental or Saastal has struck its blows in the Caucasus, Himalayas or in the American Rockies. The really old type of guide is now quite legendary and nobody can remember the waving beards of Melchior Anderegg, Christian Almer or Ulrich Lauener. The young Alpine guides of the present day have assumed all

Leontopodium alpinum (Edelweiss).

the attributes of their fathers and have been grounded in the advanced school of modern rock and ice technics. The coming generation of mountaineers look to them. It will be their role to maintain the established tradition of the calling of Swiss Alpine guide.

These guides have to pass several severe examinations and they are also given instructions regarding their duties towards the customers. Most guides understand perfectly the rules of mountain etiquette. But the tourist must do his share. He should treat his guide as a comrade not as a subordinate. However, he should not be offended if his guide rather puff at his pipe than indulge in idle chatter. The guide naturally knows more about weather and conditions in the mountains than the tourist and all decisions touching on such matters should be left to him. Fees are approved by the Swiss Alpine Club and by the government of the canton in question. And the usual 10 % tip is naturally appreciated.

Alpinism demands training. Only a hardened body will enjoy climbing. All kinds of sports serve as good preparation, but the best training remains alpinism itself. To hire a guide for a fairly long period, to discuss with him a program that leads from easy tasks to more difficult ones, that is the simplest way to become a good mountain climber. In this way alpinism will become a source of joy and health. Those wonderful hours spent in the solitude of the mountains will remain locked in the memory forever.

Yet for those who cannot afford the luxury of a guide there is still a wealth of pleasure hidden in the Alps, whether one climbs merely in search of the myriad Alpine flowers—the edelweiss, gentians, dwarf rhododendrons, saxifraga or white dryas—or whether one takes any of the many mountain railways—to the Jungfraujoch, to Muottas Muraigl, or up to the Gornergrat—in search of the magnificent views and the sense of majesty and dignity conveyed by the Alps. Twenty-seven Alpine passes are open to automobiles and on nearly all of these the official yellow post busses carry passengers as well as mail. And naturally a trip over any of these passes tends to complete one's knowledge of the Alps.

But naturally such pleasures as those provided by crag or glacier climbing can only be known by those willing to go through a fairly long and severe period of training.

« One golden summer morning you will attack the crag, » says a little book published by the Swiss Tourist Office. The guide takes the rope

from his rucksack and adjusts a firmly-knotted noose around your waist. « Shall we start? » he asks. And before you know it, he is standing where previously his hand rested, on the vertical, and as you had thought, absolutely smooth rock. Looking more closely, you observe under his nailed boot a narrow rugged projection. The nails hold fast in a minute indent-

The Jungfrau group in the Bernese Alps.

ation just large enough to accommodate half the sole of his shoe. This is a foothold; and there, where he is now gripping with his fingers, must be another small scar in the rocks serving as a handhold. Henceforward these footholds and handholds govern your pushing your body slowly up the rocky wall. This entails no risk, because the guide always climbs forward whilst you observe him. Then he tightens the rope without pulling you and you have a sense of absolute security as you place the edge of your shoe in the footholds. Should your foot slip, all that could happen would be that you would find yourself hanging motionless on the rope until your hands and feet could find another hold. You will very soon discover that you possess a particular safeguard yourself in addition to the guide's rope; whenever one hand and both feet or both hands and one foot, have a firm hold in the rock you can reach the next foothold or handhold with certainty, so that even if you were to slip from a hold there would still be two effective anchorages available. In these quite informal lessons on the steep face of the crag, you learn how to seize a handhold correctly, to control hand and foot alternately and simultaneously to give proper attention to the rope. The way in which you take up the slack, the way in which your eye follows the guide, indicate even on the first day of climbing that you have become a member of a brotherhood. Of course you will learn much in the course of the years which a practice crag cannot possibly offer. You will gradually get to know the types of rock, the angular granite, the splintering mica-schist, the smooth lime-stone boiler-plate and the crumbling gri-

stone which is, unfortunately, only too frequently intermixed with rock on which one can get a hold. As to whether you make a start climbing in nailed boots or in more flexible climbing boots, is less important than that you should be able to judge where the line of least resistance lies, where you can get a firm handhold and where care must be taken that no stone becomes detached. In the course of years you will learn to know the difference between difficulty and danger. A climb may be easy but dangerous. Then you must search for other ways up the crag, possibly difficult ones which demand all the energy you have to give but which do not have any treacherous stones.

Glacier climbing is another form of alpinism which can never be undertaken alone. However beautiful and majestic the névés and glaciers appear, they have a malign character and the experienced mountaineer never ventures on them alone. The roping of three or four men together is the best means of obviating the danger of fissures. Progress is easy on the snowless part of the ice tongue. The green abysses yawn, but one circumvents them along their

edges, crossing frequently over ice ribs no more than a foot wide, one's only concern being to get a firm foothold. This is achieved either by means of properly cut steps or by using well gripping crampons. But the contest with the invisible commences up in the region of the névé. To the unpracticed climber the latter appears to be a perfectly smooth expanse, but the eye of the guide takes in all the nuances of the surface and combines them into a whole from the position of which he is able to identify the course of the chasms. Where the eye no longer suffices, instinct provides the guide with that « awareness » of the invisible which is a sixth sense possessed by all who live close to nature. The rope becomes the principal safeguard on this tramp over crevasses which have been covered by snowdrifts. It serves as a span from man to man, like an extended arm always ready to help. Should a snowbridge suddenly collapse, the one who falls through is held by the rope. It is true that this alone does not obviate the danger completely, because to be hauled up again to the surface requires a skilful disposition of the men on the rope, much experience in getting a hold and very considerable physical strength. Those who have never set foot alone where crevasses abound, who have always been on a slack rope and associated with reliable companions, may have long and eventful experiences on glaciers and névés without ever being confronted with the problem of the crevasse. But once in, no amount of theoretical mountaineering is as useful as the helping hand at the top.

In the regular mountaineering schools you will be taught to master difficulties on absolutely safe slopes, difficulties which you may never encounter in reality, but which you should understand in order to be a confident mountaineer.

The actual mountaineering season runs from June through August, but nevertheless September and October are splendid months in the cragclimbing districts.

The Swiss Alpine Club (S. A. C.) founded in 1863 has 84 branches and over 30,000 members. The S.A.C. is responsible for having opened up the Swiss Alps so extensively by means of Club Huts as well as by the organization of guides and the publication of literature. Anyone wishing to become a member should apply to one of the S.A.C. branches which are found in all large mountaineering centres as well as in the Swiss towns. Membership carries important privileges such as reduced fares on mountain railways, lower charges in the Club Huts, etc.

The network of the Club Huts embraces the whole region of the Swiss

Alps. In contradistinction to those of other countries, the Swiss Club Huts are not taverns but places for accommodating climbers. The Club Hut is no hotel and only certain of the more frequented huts even have a caretaker. The sleeping accommodations are clean and there are always sufficient blankets available. And it is naturally taken for granted that everyone does his share in leaving the hut in the same condition in which he found it.

WINTER SPORTS

" We cannot be wholly devoted to one
enthusiasm without learning something about
the nature of all enthusiasms. "
Geoffrey YOUNG.

ALTHOUGH Switzerland has been
known at all times and in all
seasons as a tourist's paradise, it is
really during the winter months
that the country has a truly breathless
array of delights to offer. Beginning in
December and going right through until
April, Switzerland provides the most
satisfactory combinations of opportunities
for winter sports of any country in the
world. There is something for every
taste—skiing, skating, tobogganing, hockey.
Even for those people who do not indulge
in sports, Switzerland in winter is an ideal vacation sport. With its wealth of
resorts, its hotels and pensions fitted to the needs of every pocketbook,
its sun which lends to the days an almost summery warmth, it is really
what it has so often been described as—Shangri-la. Pine woods, singing
birds, blue skies and lovely snow-decked mountains—who would not
rather be in Switzerland than in the grey, foggy cities of the rest of Europe?
It is no wonder that whereas, once upon a time, everyone took his vacations in
summer, winter vacations have now become even more popular. It is not
only that one's thoughts turn to the idea of a winter vacation in Switzerland when the first snow falls, it is that from one year to the next such a
vacation has become the dream of thousands of people.

As a matter of fact, the whole development of Switzerland as a winter sports
centre is of fairly recent date. At the turn of the century, the only famous
Swiss centres open in winter were Davos, St. Moritz and Grindelwald. Skiing,
now one of the world's most popular sports, has come into its own only since
the First World War. In the early years of the 20th century, skating was the
aristocrat of winter sports and the skiing pioneers were contemptuously referred
to as « plank-hoppers ». However, in those days even skating was not the
complicated and difficult sport it has since become. The English ladies and

gentlemen, who executed gliding and graceful figures in groups of four around an orange placed primly in the middle of the rink to serve as a guiding center, would doubtless have seen little relation between their favorite pastime and the sport which reached its height in the brilliant technique of Sonja Henie. When the English foursomes were chased off the rinks by sheer weight of numbers and lack of space, a new era in winter sports began. The 20th century had begun. Sport was becoming streamlined. Each year more people were doing more things. Mountain railways were opening up even the Swiss Alps and each year some new and remote district was made available to the sportsman.

All Swiss resorts have the same general facilities to offer : Ski-schools, an ice rink with an instructor for fancy skating and hockey matches on the week-ends, ski-lifts or mountain railways to the high mountains with their more difficult runs and walks or the opportunity of watching various compet-itions for the non-sportsman. There are also many excellent curling rinks in Switzerland—a sport which seems rather mild and strange to the uninitiated but whose addicts are as passionately devoted to its delicate intricacies as the most enthusiastic skiers are to the sport of their choice.

In recent years, the Swiss have been basing the ad-vertising of their winter sport resorts on the slogan, « A Whole Nation on Skis ». In reality this is not far from the truth. The minute the first snow falls in the mountains, the stations of every Swiss city are alive on Saturday afternoons with week-end skiers. And from then until long after the daffodils are out in the valleys, nobody thinks of anything except where and when they are going to ski.

But although the Swiss themselves can think of skiing in terms of a week-end of sport, for the skiers coming from other coun-tries, it is a question of selecting the months when there is the greatest chance of having ideal snow and weather conditions.

Unquestionably the month of February is

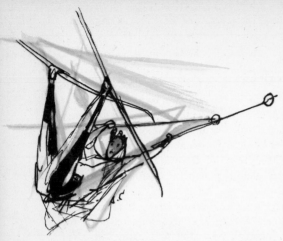

the safest month to choose. In February, there is certain to be snow everywhere. It is the month when there is the greatest chance of having a series of sunny days —but if sun is more important than anything else to anyone planning a vacation in Switzer‹land, March and even the early weeks of April are apt to be ideal in the higher resorts. Although the season opens everywhere around the 15th of December, snow conditions are apt to be uncertain until Christmas and the month of January may be pretty cold. However, anyone choosing a moment when the snow and weather conditions may not be so ideal, has the advantage of finding the mountain railroads less crowded and the slopes more to oneself.

The selection of a resort is purely a matter of individual taste—not only as far as the social life is concerned but also for skiing. Davos, St. Moritz, Wengen, Mürren, Kleine Scheidegg and Zermatt are the choices offered to the experts. But Gstaad, Villars, Arosa, Lenzerheide, Engelberg, Grindel‹wald and Klosters—to name only a few among many—all have their special attraction. And Arosa in particular is a favorite with the Swiss themselves.

In all the resorts there are ski‹schools with instruction given in at least three languages and classes ranging from beginners up through the racing classes. These schools have expert instructors and give courses with reduced rates for a certain number of lessons. The regular school hours are usually between ten and twelve in the morning and two and four in the afternoon. And although some enthusiasts attend both morning and afternoon sessions, most people choose one or the other. There are also children's classes, but humiliating as it is for the adults, children learn so much faster that they shoot through one class after another with disheartening rapidity until they reach the racing class, often while their parents who started skiing at the same time as they did are still stemming cautiously down the « nursery slopes » whose gentle graduations still seem like cliffs to them.

The ski-schools also give tests which are rewarded by bronze, silver and gold medals. By the time the gold medal has been achieved, the recipient is ready to enter the ever increasing class of good skiers. But still there is a wide gap between being just a good skier and an international racer. Ski-racing is a very special sport, for not only does it require great athletic

skill but it also pre-supposes a certain attitude of mind. Peter Lunn, himself an international racer, has vividly described this attitude of mind : « On the day of the race itself I would climb to the start in a condition of appalling nervousness, wondering why on earth I endured such misery and wishing never to race again. I do not think this nervousness can be described as stage fright because everybody seemed to suffer from it before the straight race but nobody did before the slalom one had to compete solo in front of a very large crowd. The conclusion from which is that a very large part of one's nervousness before the straight race was simply due to physical fear. The racer had made up his mind to follow a particular line and that line inevitably entailed certain risks. It is true that the racer had almost certainly taken exactly the same line in practice, but there he had been able to choose his own moment and brace himself for the effort. But in the race he had to start at the exact moment the starter told him. He was no longer a free agent but was caught in the toils of a remorseless organization. I was never one of those who found that all nervousness departed as soon as the starter had said « los ». I was always uneasy on the top slopes, in fact I was always uneasy until I had faced the worst slope of the course. This normally came about half-way down and could be considered the crisis of the race. If I held my line there, I was filled with such confidence and happiness that all subsequent hazards seemed easy. » In other words, a ski-racer feels all the same emotions as a beginner when faced with his first difficult descent, some-thing which ordinary mortals lose sight of when they stand watching racers coming down the mountains in perfect form at breakneck speed.

When deciding what to take in the line of clothes for a vacation in Switzer-land in winter, it is helpful to know a bit about what one will really need. In all the larger hotels such as the Palace Hotels in the various resorts, the guests usually dress for dinner in full evening dress and at any rate change out of their ski-clothes, whereas in the smaller hotels and pensions, one usually dines in ski-clothes or slacks. However, even if one is planning to stay in a small hotel or pension, it is better to take evening clothes along—for there is sure to be some gala which one will want to attend. But for the daytime, ski-clothes are all that anyone needs—ski clothes and a good, warm coat.

In addition to skating and skiing, tobogganing is another favorite winter sport in Switzerland. But like both the other sports, tobogganing also had its mild and gentle beginnings, when invalids who had gone to Davos for their health took it up in a very simple and amateurish way. However, it was not long before the invalids were outclass-ed and had to watch, rather resentfully, the sportsmen of all nations catapulting down the Cresta Run at St. Moritz at hair-raising speeds or on bob-sled teams banking high on the hairpin turn at Sunny Corner.

Another sport, but one which has more spectators than followers, is ski-jumping and each winter international competitions

Davos in winter.

are held in Switzerland. As a matter of fact, to become a Swiss ski-champion, it is necessary to be not only a downhill racer, but a slalom expert, good in the «Langlauf», which is a regular marathon on skis, and to be able to jump as well. The championship is decided on a combination of points in these very different fields of skiing.

St. Moritz is without question the best-known Swiss resort, due partly to the fact that here are located such a large number of huge hotels and partly to the fact that it has always been popular with international society. Certainly anyone interested in the fashionable side of winter sports must pay at least one visit to St. Moritz and to the world famous bar of the Palace Hotel. The skiing is good at St. Moritz but not as popular with the experts as the skiing at Davos. The runs in St. Moritz are short

and steep and the Corviglia Railway takes one to the top in about fifteen minutes. From here there is a good choice of runs down into St. Moritz or to Celerina as well as a chance of cutting across to the ski-lift by the Suvretta Hotel which, like the Corviglia Railway, takes you to a point where you have a choice of runs. Both at the top of the Corviglia and half way down there are restaurants with sunny terraces and most skiers make a day of it, ordering their lunch at their hotels or pensions and then getting a plate of soup or an accompanying bottle of wine in the various eating-places scattered over the slopes. All Swiss hotels put up picnic lunches which, replacing a regular lunch, are included in the general price arrangement. Everyone who goes to Davos, whether he is a skier or not, must take the railway up to Weissfluhjoch on a sunny day and lunch on the terrace with its magnificent panorama of snow-covered Alps and its crowds of skiers shooting down what look to the laymen like impossibly steep slopes. It has been said that the terrace of the restaurant at Weissfluhjoch is one place where, if you sit there long enough, everyone in the world will walk by. And truly no one who has not seen this starting point of the great Parsenn ski-runs can quite understand the lure and thrill that lies in skiing. If anyone is determined to resist this most fascinating of all sports, he better stay away from the Parsenn. Here is where even the most stubborn opponents of the sport succumb and go sneaking off themselves to buy a pair of skis.

Skiing in Davos dates back to the last century. At that time Tobias Branger of Davos who had gone as a saddler's apprentice to Paris saw a pair of skis in the Norwegian section of the World's Fair of 1878. It occurred to him that these skis might prove to be pretty useful in his own snow-covered country. But he forgot all about them temporarily. However a pair of skis actually appeared in 1888 in Davos when a Colonel Napier who was living in a chalet near the village had a Norwegian valet who had a pair of skis and went skiing about the village on them. He skied very nicely and people began to tell tales of his exploits, how for instance he had carried a tray full of things down to the hotel without falling. But in a way he was regarded as something of a clown and when he left the village and gave his skis to someone else, they were never used. Then Tobias Branger returned from his apprenticeship in France and told his brother, a passionate mountaineer, about the skis he had seen in Paris. They decided to send to Norway for a pair, but when the skis eventually arrived, they had much difficulty in learning to use them and the natives made such fun of the two brothers that they had to do their practising at night. But by the time they had become expert enough so that they were able to travel over the pass to Arosa and back, even the natives began to see some sense to these queer pieces of wood. Then in 1894, Sir Arthur Conan Doyle came to Davos. He had read Nansen's book on Greenland and he had a vague idea of what skiing was like. The Branger brothers helped show him how to manage a

pair of skis. For weeks they practised together, for in those days before the development of a specialized technique, it took weeks to learn what can now be learned in a few minutes. They all took some short trips together and Conan Doyle, when he returned to England, described these trips. Gradually more and more people became interested in the sport and, with the opening of the Parsenn Railway, Davos became a teeming anthill of skiers. The following are some of the runs from Weissfluh to Davos : Standard, Dorfberg, Dorftäli. They are all rather difficult and should not be attempted unless one is a fairly good skier. The Meierhoftäli, which ends at Wolfgang from where a train must be taken back to Davos, is a very popular run with good skiers, particularly in the late winter months. The top part of the run is a lovely, open « schuss » usually with excellent snow conditions, but the lower part of the run has a tricky stretch of woods which is difficult for any but very good skiers. As a matter of fact, the whole Parsenn district requires a fairly high level of skiing. The easiest of all the runs is the Strela with its ski-lift and its own funicular starting from Davos Platz.

The Parsenn runs which lead down to Küblis, Fideris, Klosters and Serneus are not as difficult as the runs to Davos, but they are very much longer with

restaurants half way down where ordinary mortals stop for lunch or for an hour's sun in the campchairs on the terraces and where even those speed demons who have to make several eleven or twelve mile runs in a day con, descend to stop for a drink. The run to Küblis, on which the Parsenn Derby is held annually, is a famous racing run with wonderful open country on most of its eleven mile expanse. While the run to Klosters, which is the same as the Küblis run in its upper stretches, has a wood path after the Klosters Schwendi restaurant which is situated more than half way down the run.

Mürren, Wengen and Grindelwald have splendid ski runs which are not as long and difficult as those of the Parsenn but which offer a wider variety than those of St. Moritz. Kleine Scheidegg, with its one large hotel but no village, is a very popular resort from Christmas till early spring and it is in the spring that Zermatt becomes the mecca of all enthusiasts driven by the melting snows from other resorts.

The Matterhorn towering above the surrounding mountains dominates the narrow valley, which, running from its foot north and south, houses the village of Zermatt. Zermatt is composed of the old native village with its wooden chalets and of modern hotels and villas. The slopes of the valley are covered with woods, very thick on the northern slopes but thinning out somewhat on the southern ones. Sheltered by the surrounding mountains from the violence of southern and northern winds, the valley is an ideal spot for skiing. Snow generally covers the beautiful slopes surrounding Zermatt around the end of November and only disappears around the middle of May. However, in the im, mediate neighborhood of Zermatt there is snow all the year round and skiing can be enjoyed even in the long warm days of August here as it can be high on the Jungfrau. Nevertheless the winter months are naturally the best for skiing. During December, January and Fe, bruary, Zermatt is generally less popular with tourists than during the next two or three spring months. The days get longer and warmer, while the snow on the well protected northern slopes retains its perfect winter condi,

tions sometimes up until the middle of April. In the spring Zermatt offers to all mountain lovers an incredible variety of attractions. Not only can the skier follow the long, easy trails which cut the mountain side in all directions, but availing himself of the generally safe atmospheric conditions, he may venture for long excursions all through the fantastically beautiful country which surrounds the little village.

Zermatt has a ski-lift and a mountain railway. The ski-lift which starts at the beginning of the village takes skiers in about 20 minutes to a place called « Blau-herd » some few hundred feet above timberline where the southern sun shines even in January from the earliest hours of the morning onward. From « Blauherd » there are a number of runs down to Zermatt. Three of these are the most popular and the ones which are the goal of the average skier. Two of them run down towards Zermatt through wide, even tracks cut into the woods. These tracks offer to any skier all the thrills and

pleasure he may seek. One, called the Standard, is an easy run, popular with beginners and often with experienced skiers who like it because of its possibilities of affording a very fast run. The Standard, which starts at the top station of the ski-lift, in the open meadow, with an easy, pleasant « schuss » gradually enters the thick woods twisting around a 60 ft. wide trail. This run takes the skier down to Zermatt through a continuous series of small « schusses » and flat runs, connected to each other by long wide curves. The average skier can take it leisurely and be down in between 40 and 50 minutes while a good skier can « schuss » down the four mile run in a little over 5 minutes. Both will end up at the little shack which houses the ski-lift station.

Another run is known, for some mysterious reason, as « Rio de Janeiro ». For the first mile the skier follows the easy Standard, then suddenly he leaves the easy slopes and goes down a very steep « schuss » which from above looks very much like a precipice. This run is about a mile and a half long, but every inch of it is thrilling. It is steep, rugged and fast. Only experienced skiers can go down this way, but when they do even they have a thrill. Skiers must « parallel » down from right to left in a constant slalom which, even if not as binding as a real one, is just as exciting and quite as hard.

Still another run leads back to a little village called Findelen, the highest inhabited village in Europe. One skis down to Findelen through wide open meadows and from Findelen to Zermatt through an easy, yet quite interesting trail which winds between the trunks of century old pine trees.

But the ski-lift is only one of the many assets of Zermatt. The village also boasts of a railway which is one of the highest in the world which takes you in a little over 40 minutes from Zermatt to the Gornergrat. This railway runs a number of well heated trains up and down all day in order to allow eager skiers the chance to repeat those runs they like a good number of times. It stops at four intermediate stations, Riffelalp, Riffelboden, Riffelberg and Roten-Boden. And skiers may catch the next train at any of these stations.

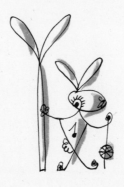

FISHING

« Oh! the brave Fisher's life,
It is the best of any,
It's full of pleasure, void of strife
And it's beloved of many. »
Izaak WALTON, « The Compleat Angler ».

ISHING, like hunting, has always been one of the privileges of free men. Consequently, it is only natural that in Switzerland fishing is a very popular sport. Small as the country is, with an area of only 16,000 sq. miles, it has a surface area of 160,000 hectares of water, of which 135,000 hectares are in lakes and ponds. The total length of its rivers and streams is the distance from San Francisco to Japan via Europe.

The most cherished dream of any angler who has previously cast his fly into the waters of the Swiss rivers, is to return as soon as possible to again enjoy the pleasant and gratifying experience.

The Orbe river noted for its ten pound trout, the Reuss with its twenty pound fish, the Rhone where countless rainbows trout are awaiting him, to say nothing of the Inn, the Plessur, the Landquart, the Grande Eau, the Doubs, or the many quiet and turbulent streams that everywhere grace the Swiss countryside.

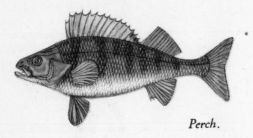

Perch.

More than fifty thousand Swiss citizens indulge in the sport of fishing annually and at least three hundred families earn their living by it. The annual catch is estimated at 2 millions kilos, which represents a value of 5 million francs. The greater part, about 1,300,000 kilos, is from the lakes and is caught by professional fishermen, while about 50 pisciculture establishments furnish approximately 200,000 kilos.

The number of fish in each lake varies : 31 kilos per hectare in the lake of Lugano, 17 kilos per hectare in the lake of Zurich, 5 kilos per hectare in

Brochet.

lake Leman, etc. The figures for the rivers and streams show still greater variety. Of course this does not depend only on natural conditions, but on a more or less methodic exploitation and on restocking.

In one year, the lakes and streams in Switzerland were restocked with 16,500,000 trout, 1,000,000 sommerling trout, and 1,208,000 rainbow trout by the State alone.

In addition, there is re-stocking through private initiative.

These figures show what a matter of solicitude fishing is to the authorities, who in return expect the fishermen to adhere scrupulously to the rules which are handed him when he obtains his licence.

Owing to the fact that the cantons have sovereign rights, these rules may vary slightly but only within the limits imposed by the Federal law.

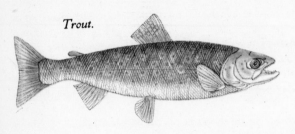

Trout.

Every fisherman is expected to keep an exact and honest account of his catch, for only in this way can a rationally organized pisciculture be developed. During the early spring, the fishing is best in the Jura or in the Valais. Later comes the season for Tessin, while in the summer months there is a wealth of choice in the high Alps.

There are many varieties of fish in Switzerland, from the ordinary trout to the ombre and ombre-chevalier. Then there are feras, brochets, carps, perches, lottes and a vast number of lesser varieties.

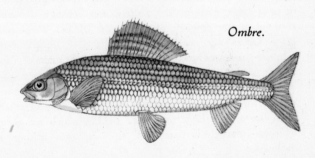

Ombre.

The fresh water trout (salmo fario) is the sport fish par excellence. It is found in the rivers as well as in the streams but has a preference for cold and turbulent waters, strongly oxygenated. It is found up to an altitude of 6,000 feet.

The Naymacush and rainbow trout are found only in the higher Alpine lakes of the Valais, Berne and the Grisons. These two varieties are great fighters and very popular with fisherman.

The lake trout (salmo lacustris) are much longer, attaining sometimes a weight of 20 pounds. But these fish are more difficult and belong to the catch of the professional fishermen.

The famous Cristivomer, the big, grey Canadian trout which weighs as much as 40 pounds has been successfully acclimatized in a few of the mountain lakes.

The ombre and the brochet can be found throughout Switzerland up to an altitude of 3,200 feet.

The ordinary ombre (Thymallus Thymallus) is found in many rivers. The fishermen who have had the opportunity of fighting it consider this sport as most fascinating.

This fish, extremely prudent, is an indefatigable fighter, the King of the swift waters.

And naturally perch are to be found in all the larger lakes.

Wading is not widely practised but, where it is, the fishermen wear thigh high boots rather than real waders.

Fly fishing is a joy in Switzerland. As soon as the water is no longer clouded by the melting snow (6,000 feet), the trout begin to rise to flies. There is also a great choice of insects. The Mayfly can be found from the 20th of May on, and the baetis, the ecdyures and the phryganides are also used for bait.

A wide choice of artificial flies is not needed as the classical ones succeed in most cases, such as the : *Olive dun, molesfly, Banama, Cowsdung,* (Switzerland is the country of cows), the *Alder, Wickham's fancy, Greenwalls glory, Red spinner,* etc.

In many streams however the trout will only strike at a special kind of insect and it is best to ask the natives regarding this point.

Fly fishing can be enjoyed in many rivers; it is especially successful after sunset, for, in the daytime, the waters are very clear and the trout hide from the intense light under the pebbles which are always very numerous in these places. In most of the cantons, fishing is authorized till darkness.

Of course there are nearly as many different kind of fishermen as there are varieties of fish—each one showing his own particular inclination and preference.

These range from the professional fishermen, a modest, hardworking and courageous lot—for the Swiss lakes are subject to sudden tempests and it is no joke to manipulate the nets on a stormy night—to the tribe of placid creatures one sees by every lakeside, staring blankly into the water or puffing contentedly at their pipes; from the nature lovers—who spend delightful hours near a mountain lake whose monster-haunted depths no sounding-lead ever reached—to the mere « gourmets » who expect more pleasure from a good dinner of fresh fish dripping with butter and cream, before a glass of the prime wine of the country, than from any glorious catch.

SWISS INDUSTRY

AND
TECHNICAL SCIENCE

Switzerland is a land of inventors.

It leads all other countries in the percentage of patents issued in proportion to the population. Not only does the Federal Institute of Technology in Zurich do a great deal of industrial research work, but all the big industrial corporations have their own laboratories as well. Many Nobel prizes for research have gone to Swiss.

Basel's harbour, on the Rhine.

LOOKING at the clean towns and pleasant villages of Switzerland, many travellers wonder what the Swiss people do for a living. Sometimes the Swiss wonder themselves. In former days, Switzerland was mainly an agricultural country, exploiting her forests and grazing-lands, cultivating cereals and the vine. The small-farmer class, which today forms one-quarter of the population, has always constituted one of the most vital forces of the nation. But although agriculture is still a necessary and important factor in Swiss economic life, during the past century, Switzerland has created an industrial structure which has now become an essential element of her prosperity. Industry absorbs 45 % of the nation's workers, while agriculture accounts for only 22 %.

Thanks to the nation's spirit of enterprise, technical skill and methodical organization, Switzerland holds an economic importance relatively far superior to her size. Throughout the Jura region, in Geneva, Schaffhausen, Glarus and St. Gall, still more in and around Zurich and Basel, there are factories and manufacturing plants employing almost a million workers.

As Switzerland has practically no natural resources, Swiss industry must buy raw materials on foreign markets and export its products in payment of its purchases.

The oldest of the many industries in Switzerland is the textile industry for which the raw wool and cotton as well as the silk cocoons have to be imported. Switzerland was one of the first countries in Europe to manufacture silks, laces and embroideries. And in this respect Zurich has always been a rival of Lyon and Milan, while Basel is famous thoughout the world for its ribbons.

Cotton spinning and weaving were introduced into Switzerland in the 17th century and today this flourishing industry centres in the cantons of St. Gall, Glarus and Zurich with branches specializing in embroidery and lace in Thurgau, St. Gall and Appenzell. It is also in the canton of Appenzell that the finest hand embroidery is still done. The knitting and hosiery trade, the linen industry, even the manufacture of shoes, are all considered a part of the textile industry. Swiss shoes have always been an item of importance in the salons of the Paris designers.

At Wohlen, in the canton of Aargau, twenty-five firms are occupied with the manufacture and sale of straw for hats and are considered as a branch of the textile trade.

Yet, despite the prominence of the textile trade, with its various branches, it is the heavy industries which hold first place—founderies, steel works, machine plants of all kinds—a position they share with the electro-technical group, famed for its turbines, generators and motors.

Switzerland has done much pioneering in the field of electricity. Its water-power is largely exploited. Not only are railroads, foundries and factories supplied with electricity but so is every house in the country, with the exception of remote stables and shelters in the high Alps.

The abundance of electric power plays an important role in the machine industry. This industry makes electrical equipment, water and steam turbines, motors, locomotives, high frequency switches, etc.

Engineers of Sulzer Brothers in Winterthur have developed Diesel engines for ocean transport. All over the world, Diesel motors for ships are built according to plans laid in Winterthur, although Winterthur lies far from the sea.

The electrical industry provides a wide choice of products covering the generation, transmission, distribution and application of electrical energy. Owing to its size, the Swiss electrical industry is able to export a high proportion of its products in addition to supplying the needs of the home market.

In the middle of the war, Brown Boveri perfected the gas turbine locomotive. The most modern steam engine needs a ton of coal and nine tons of water to generate as much power as a gas turbine engine will produce on half a ton of crude oil. The additional 125 tons of air needed naturally do not weigh on the engine because it does not have to haul them.

A particularly progressive invention of recent date is the heat pump plant, a form of inverted refrigerator. Small quantities of heat are drawn from waste steam or even any running water on hand and pumped to a temperature high enough for practical uses. The biggest heat pump plant in Switzerland is in the Rhine Salt Works. The biggest one in the world, that evaporates 10 tons of water an hour, is in a foreign aluminium works. Both were built by Escher‹Wyss of Zurich. Escher‹Wyss also developed the variable pitch propeller to brake the speed of airplanes when landing.

Every type of machine and accessory used in the textile trade can be supplied by Swiss firms and long years of experience have made these firms authorities in this field.

Another important group which has shown marked and rapid progress during the last twenty years is the machine tool industry.

The Swiss automobile industry is well‹known for its heavy and semi‹heavy lorries. Other important industrial products are machinery for flour mills and for the food industries, paper‹making machines, printing presses, packing machinery, agricultural machinery, optical and surveying instruments, meters, counters and typewriters.

Naturally the watch industry, which today extends from Geneva to Schaff‹hausen, will always be one of the principal industries of Switzerland and one with which the name of the country will remain most closely bound. In the course of generations, a numerous population has acquired great technical aptitude and a justly renowned skill. A tradition has thus been created by which the trade is so strongly rooted in the life of the population that even when times are bad, confidence is never shaken.

The jeweller's art is centred principally in Geneva, where a large number of specialists—engravers, enamellers, gold and silversmiths—have brought their work to a high level of perfection.

One other important Swiss industry is the chemical industry centering around Basel. Dye firms are situated in Basel while there are large concerns specializing in the manufacture of pharmaceutical products in Basel, Zofingen, Berne and St. Gall.

Names of Swiss chemical or pharmaceutical firms such as Hoffmann-La-Roche, Ciba and Geigy are famous throughout the world. DDT, a power which kills all insects and yet is non-toxic to man was invented by Geigy.

Certain products such as sulphuric acid have been made in Switzerland for over 100 years, while sodium chloride has for a long time been obtained from the Rhine salt beds and at Bex.

The electro-chemical industry embraces enterprises whose products differ widely, but whose manufacture has the common feature that a chemical conversion process by the direct action of electric energy is used. Among electro-chemically manufactured products, aluminium takes a leading place. It is made at Neuhausen, Chippis and Martigny and worked up in various factories. Apart from aluminium, metallic sodium (at Monthey) and iron alloys (Visp, Bex, Bodio) are manufactured electro-chemically.

The food and tobacco industries, chocolate manufacture, the production of cheese and condensed milk, the products of the Nestlé concern, the pre-serving industry, the ceramic and paper industry, as well as the graphic arts, all flourish in Switzerland and contribute to making the standard of living in this country what it is. Furthermore the zipper is a Swiss invention, and the Swiss were the first to use tar to pave roads and to solve the problem of liquefying coal.

INDEX OF TOWNS AND PLACES

272